IDEAS FOR YOUR GARDEN IN COLOUR

ROB HERWIG
With the co-operation of Wolfram Stehling, photographer

IDEAS FOR YOUR GARDEN IN COLOUR

Translated by Marian Powell

LUTTERWORTH PRESS • GUILDFORD AND LONDON

Line drawings: Rob Herwig

Photographs: Wolfram Stehling
          Rob Herwig (pp. 27, 32, 49, 65, 75, 85, 86, 91, 97, 101)

First published in Great Britain in 1975

ISBN 0 7188 2176 9

Filmset by Keyspools Ltd., Golborne, Lancs.

Printed in the Netherlands

CONTENTS

INTRODUCTION

Increased awareness and appreciation of our remaining environment has led to heightened interest in gardening. Since in many cases gardening starts with the construction or re-designing of the garden or part of it, a certain demand for information on this subject has made itself felt, a demand not easy to satisfy, for there is as yet a great lack of suggestions for garden lay-out in book form. Hence this little volume.

In compiling this work I have chosen mainly practical examples as guidelines. In other words, no extravagant concepts, difficult to put into effect, but chiefly very realisable ideas. At the same time I have tried to avoid the commonplace, for if you want the kind of garden of which there are thirteen to the dozen, you would probably not have bought this book. I would advise you not to allow yourself to be frustrated if, at first sight, some of the ideas illustrated seem rather difficult; they are all perfectly feasible — otherwise I would not have chosen them!

To clarify the technical aspects to some extent, the book starts with a number of hints concerning construction, so that an amateur, reasonably proficient in 'do-it-yourself' can himself carry out the ideas. Apart from the text and the photographs, the fifty ideas are further explained in simple sketches. If you do not want to do the work yourself, all this may be used to make your requirements clear to someone else — leave it to you.

In any case I wish you a great deal of pleasure and success in designing or improving your garden.

Rob Herwig

DESIGNING YOUR GARDEN

...rst draw your plan

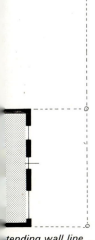

...tending wall line

Put it down on paper

If you start to dig and build in your garden without a definite plan, you will almost certainly encounter unpleasant surprises. The measurements may not be exactly as you thought; when the work is finished you may regret not having done it quite differently. It is rather like a photograph, of which an expert says that it should have been taken from a slightly different angle . . . A photograph can easily be taken again, but the same hardly applies to a garden. Hence my first tip: start by putting everything neatly down on paper.

This is in any case not a difficult job. It is easiest to work with faintly printed graph paper with 1×1-cm ($\frac{1}{2} \times \frac{1}{2}$-in.) squares. You can also draw the squares yourself, for instance in blue on white paper. Next you mark all fixed points in black, such as house-walls, windows and doors, existing trees, the boundaries of the garden, etc. In many cases the basic details may be copied from architectural drawings, but be sure to check these, for often the dimensions of the site, in particular, have been incorrectly marked.

To simplify matters you can stick to a scale of 1:100, especially for an average-sized garden. Small gardens or details are usually drawn to a slightly larger scale, for example 1:50.

Measurements are important

In the case of a small garden a yardstick is sufficient to check an existing drawing. Larger areas, say, above 10 m (11 yd), are best measured with a measuring tape; a 3-m (10-ft) tape is quite suitable for amateurs.

If no plan is available, but the house wall is there, you can 'transpose' the façade with the aid of two straight slats and one open eye. The furthest slat is placed in line with the house wall and the distance can be measured once more. To proceed it is necessary to construct a second line at a square angle with the sighting line. If you have ever done any geometry, you will realise that this is not at all difficult, either on paper or in the garden.

Using three lengths of string, one of 3, one of 4 and one of 5 m (3, 4, 5 yd), we are once again going to prove the theorem of Pythagoras (see sketch). Knot the ends together, making a loop. Place two small posts along the existing

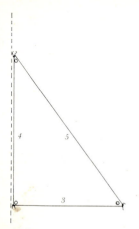

Making a right angle

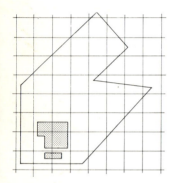

Charting an irregularly shaped garden

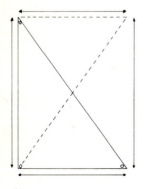

Checking a right angle

straight line and put the string round them in such a manner that the knots at the ends of the 4-m (4-yd) piece touch the posts. If you now place the third post at the third knot, you will have a line at a square angle. If necessary this line can be extended again, and in this way you can cover the entire garden, however irregular its shape, with a network of square angled lines, giving the correct measurements.

If you are not very familiar with this type of work, it is advisable to check that the angles are accurate. This can be done very simply by reversing the knotted pieces of string (see dotted line). You should thus obtain a rectangle with sides of exactly 3 (3) and 4 m (4 yd). Check with your tape and correct if necessary.

A garden at different levels

A garden is not always perfectly level; what is more, it is not desirable to have it so. In small gardens especially, it is the cleverly created differences in level, however slight, which contribute so much to improving the spatial effect. A cursory examination of this book will prove my point.

Right, so we want to play about with levels. But how do we determine the differences in height?

If you possess a spirit level and a perfectly straight board or slat, 2–3 m (2–3 yd) in length, it will be child's play. The threshold of the garden door is usually taken as the starting point. We call this level 0·00. If you lay one end of the board or slat on the threshold (on its side, please!), placing the spirit level on top, you can hold it in such a way that the zero level is transferred 2–3 m (2–3 yd). Hammer a stake into the ground at this point, or stack a number of bricks, and place the other end of the board on top. The air bubble in the spirit level should now be exactly in the centre. From this new zero level you continue until the entire garden is covered in posts marking the 0·00 level. If the distance between the soil and the top of a stake is 30 cm (1 ft), the level at this point $-0·30$ m ($-\frac{1}{3}$ yd). Simple, isn't it?

Of course the garden may slope upwards instead of downwards. When this is the case, you extend the last stake before the bump by 50 or 100 cm (20 or 40 in.) and continue as before. If you have lengthened the stake by 100 cm (40 in.), and the distance between the ground and the top of the next stake is again 30 cm (1 ft), the level at this point $+0·70$ cm ($+28$ in.).

If you like you can accurately chart the exact outlines of the garden surface. As a rule this is unnecessary and it is sufficient

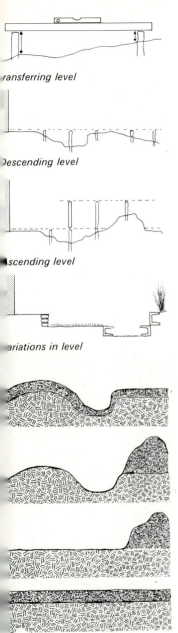

Transferring level

Descending level

Ascending level

Variations in level

Levelling: keep topsoil separate

to determine the level at a number of important points, for instance, in the sunken seating area, on the paths, or a bank.

Moving soil

If you should decide to put one or more of the ideas in this book into practice, it will in nine cases out of ten involve moving soil. You've decided on a sunken area; foundations must be laid for a path; it does not take long to decide, but it all involves many barrow-loads.

This does not matter, provided you can get rid of the soil elsewhere, and that preferably near at hand, for instance in your own garden. In other words, if you plan a sunken seating area, plan a mound as well, where you can put the soil. You need not go to such lengths that you have to make a hill at any price, just because you wish to get rid of soil. But if it is at all possible (and really, this is often the case), try not to take soil out of your garden. It will save you an enormous amount of work, or, if you are having the job done by someone else, money.

If your garden is already established there will be a layer of so-called topsoil, in which organic life takes place. This layer is about 40 cm (16 in.) deep and is characterised by its black colour and loose structure. The better the quality of the topsoil, the easier you can distinguish it when digging.

Sometimes the gardens of new houses contain a layer of topsoil as well; this can be seen from the vegetation or be determined after some digging. In many cases, however, the garden has been raised with worthless soil, mixed with building rubble. As a rule all this has been dumped on a hard foundation of soil rammed down by traffic and covered with a thin layer of black earth for the sake of appearances. All this should really be removed before you can make a start.

If there is a layer of good topsoil, use it economically and reserve it for those areas where you want something to grow. To give an example: if you want to raise the level at a given spot by 30 cm (12 in.), you should first remove the 40 cm (16-in.) layer of topsoil, raise the level by 30 cm (12 in.) (if necessary with poor soil) and then put back the topsoil. It's a lot of work, but it is much better for your plants. In any case, if you plan the job intelligently, it can usually be organised fairly efficiently. It's worth an evening's thought. You might draw up a work scheme, such as: soil from point A is moved to B, point A is then partly filled with rubble from point C, etc. In this way you may save yourself a lot of unnecessary work.

Work scheme for moving soil

Wall foundation

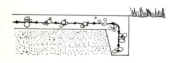

Protecting edge along concrete path

Sleeper construction

A sound foundation

Whatever you are building in the garden, be it a low wall, or a fence made from railway sleepers, you want it to last. You can achieve this by providing good foundations.

In the case of a wall, the foundation serves to spread the load over a larger area. For that reason it is wider at the bottom. The wall will remain upright only if the subsoil is firm. You will find this when digging; as a rule you will hit firm soil at a depth of about 60 cm (24 in.). If the subsoil is soft, it will be impossible to construct ordinary foundations. In such cases piles will have to be sunk, which is usually too expensive for an ordinary garden, but in general it will not be necessary to do this.

The danger of lifting as a result of frost is always mentioned in connection with foundations. What exactly does this mean? When this happens, water has collected under a foundation, which turns to ice in severe frost. Since ice takes up more room than the same quantity of water, everything will be pushed upwards with tremendous force. When the ice thaws, it will all subside again, but by that time a wall or a concrete pool will have cracked.

To prevent this happening we can do two things:
1. Make sure that no water can collect underneath the foundation.
2. Lay the foundation at frost-free level.

In the case of walls the latter solution is the easier. Frost free depth is taken to be 60–80 cm (24–32 in.). If the wall is not an expensive one and is well covered with plants at its base, 40 cm (16 in.) might be sufficient.

When constructing paths (which can suffer the same kind of damage), the former method is used, by laying a bed of rubble and sand which remains permanently dry. Concrete terraces are protected by an edge, which will keep the soil underneath the concrete relatively dry.

When you are using railway sleepers, a foundation is unnecessary, even if you do not place them at a frost-free level. The sleepers will rise, but will not be damaged. The bottom sleeper is often laid in a layer of sand by way of foundation.

Brick laying

If you want a really fine wall, you would probably do better to leave it to a professional. It is extremely difficult to build level, especially when using the concrete elements so popular nowadays (patio bricks and that sort of thing).

If you only want a low wall, or a few steps, you might have a go yourself. Mortar is made in a tub by mixing cement, sand and water, and that is quite easy. Before you start building you erect 'profiles' at each corner; these are wooden posts on which the layers of masonry are marked with a pencil. By stretching a piece of string between two marks you can keep the work level. Make sure that the mortar is not too soft, and hammer down each brick separately. Afterwards the joins are rendered with a special mortar containing silver sand.

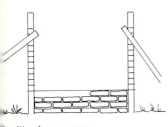

Profiles for masonry

Surplus water must be drained away

If your garden is low-lying, or if you have badly draining soil, it may happen that after a heavy downpour terraces and sunken gardens are flooded. After a time the water will disappear of its own accord, but nevertheless it can be a nuisance. This is why I usually incorporate a small outlet in a sunken area, to which the paving is made to slope slightly. By way of a plastic pipe the water drains into a rubble pit, that is, a deep hole into which all unwanted rubble has been dumped. A cubic metre (cubic yard) of rubble is more than sufficient to hold the result of a thunderstorm. The bottom of the rubble pit should be at water-level or above it.

If a fibreglass pool is temporarily used as a sandpit, this, too, will require drainage. This can be connected to the same system. Everything you need, that is, 5-cm (2-in.) pvc tubing, connecting pieces and drain boxes, can be bought from builders' merchants or do-it-yourself shops.

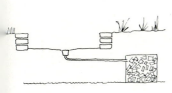

Drainage of sunken area

Be your own pavior

You don't have to, of course, but as it is usually difficult to get a pavior for a small job, it is often the only way. You might be able to find a pavior in full-time employment who is willing to do some 'moonlighting' in his spare time. Since he knows his job, he will be able to lay the stone level at the first attempt simply by using a string. For D.I.Y. jobs, and especially for untrained labour, another system has been invented in Germany, one which I can heartily recommend from my own experience. But first a word about the foundation.

As already mentioned under the heading 'A sound foundation', pavements, too, can suffer frost damage. This happens only if water can collect underneath the stones or slabs, which expands on freezing and pushes up the paving. To avoid this, paving should always be well-drained, so that

it remains dry underneath. This is best achieved by firs[t]
digging out the area to be paved to a depth of 20 cm (8 in.)
Next you put down a layer of rubble or gravel (you may wel[l]
have a lot of rubble to get rid of in any case; if not, plenty wil[l]
be found along the walls of a new house!), with a 5-cm
(2-in.) layer of coarse sand on top. This should be wel[l]
watered, so that the sand sinks between the rubble or gravel
and the entire area should then be well rammed down with [a]
wooden or iron rammer. This is important, for if the path o[r]
terrace should subside at a later stage, you would be left with
an uneven pavement.

We now come to the do-it-yourself system, which I ca[n]
best describe by taking as an example a path 1 m (1 yd) wide
The track has been prepared, watered and rammed down
Next you set wooden boards on either side of the path
attaching them at 2-m (2-yd) intervals to firm low posts
Check that the boards are level and at the same height o[n]
either side with the aid of a spirit level. Once this has bee[n]
done, you make a levelling board, that is, a plank of a certai[n]
shape which can be moved along the boards to give th[e]
layer of sand the correct outline (see sketch). You will se[e]
that the lower edge of the leveller is slightly curved; this i[s]
done to make the path convex, so that water will drain off t[o]
the sides.

At either end of the levelling board you will see an indenta-
tion; this has a purpose. The top of the edging board is leve[l]
with the top of the final pavement, which means that the
sand must be levelled at the depth of a brick. In other words
you make a 4, 5 or 6 cm ($1\frac{3}{4}$, 2 or $2\frac{1}{2}$ in.) notch at either en[d]
of the leveller.

If you have done your job properly, the sand will have bee[n]
rammed down so well that there will be a 2–4 cm ($\frac{3}{4}$–$1\frac{3}{4}$ in.)
gap under the leveller. Scatter some loose sand on top an[d]
pull the leveller gently towards you. The track will now hav[e]
the correct profile and only the thin upper layer will consist o[f]
sand, which must not be walked on before the bricks are i[n]
place.

Level the entire path in this way before you start laying the
bricks, starting at one end. Stretch a piece of string inside th[e]
planks to guide you. You may walk on a finished area, but b[e]
careful. The bricks should be placed accurately but shoul[d]
under no circumstances be hammered down.

When the path has been completed, the boards are carefully removed and the edges of the path are firmly filled with
soil. Brush some sharp sand over the length of the path and [...]

Well-drained path

Levelling the sandbed

...dging boards for levelling a ...rrace

will be ready for use. As the bricks or slabs have nowhere to go, they will stay put.

Terraces and other large areas can be paved in the same manner. Provided the levelling board is made of firm wood, it can be up to 2 m (2 yd) in length. When you have laid a 2-m (2-yd) strip, you set the next edging board, and so on. Terraces paved in a certain pattern can also be easily laid by this method, provided the material used is of even thickness. If you were to alternate, for instance, 4-cm (1¾-in.) thick washed concrete tiles with lines of red brick placed on their side — perhaps 11 cm (4½ in.) in thickness — you will encounter problems. In this case you would do best to lay everything on the levelled sand and later to remove the bricks one by one, take out some sand, and replace the bricks at the required depth.

With this method it is also much easier to achieve the slope of 2 cm per metre (¾ in. per yd), required for terraces, than by using a spirit level and a rubber hammer.

Digging loosens the soil

If you have a small garden which has already been subjected to several of the operations described above, there will be little left to dig. So much soil will already have been moved that the earth in the areas to be planted will by now be sufficiently friable.

But where the ground has not yet been worked, is covered in weeds and rubbish, and rammed down by traffic in the course of building operations, digging — preferably to a depth of two spits — is a desirable measure.

To be able to dig thoroughly, it is necessary to start by making a trench. The sketch shows a section of a two-spit trench. The soil removed is taken to the far end of the plot for the time being, making sure that the topsoil is separate from that of the second spit. The actual digging can now begin. You start by cutting away the weeds in a thin layer, which you throw upside down in the deepest part of the trench. At this level — 60 cm (24 in.) below the surface — it is unlikely that the weeds will come up again. The second spit from the next trench is thrown on top of this weed layer, and the top spit from the third trench is placed on top of everything. This completes the cycle, and you start again.

I love this job, particularly in autumn or in spring, when it isn't too hot. The soil has now been turned upside down. When you have come to the end of the strip to be dug (it is easiest if this is between 1 and 3 m (1 and 3 yd) wide), you

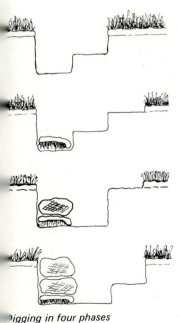

...igging in four phases

will then use the soil which you dug from the first trench.

Soil worked in this way can be left at 5–8 cm (2–3 in.) above the desired final level. In six months it will have subsided. The soil structure will be improved if after digging it can be left alone during a period of frost; this applies particularly to clay soil.

Soil improvement

Wild plants grow in the most diverse circumstances. Some are found in damp, acid soil, rich in humus, in the shade of tall trees; others flourish in high, dry and rocky situations in full sunlight. Every nurseryman's catalogue contains plants of both categories and you will find them in many gardens. How can we adapt the soil in our gardens to make it suitable for both types of plants (as well as for many others)?

This can never be a hundred per cent successful. If you want perfection, a special environment should be created for each plant, complete with special soil mixture. As a rule we do not go quite so far, but we do take into consideration that, for instance, a Rhododendron likes light shade and requires damp and acid soil. Such details are found in every good garden encyclopaedia.

A large group of shrubs, perennials and conifers are satisfied with what we might call 'average garden soil'. This may be sandy soil containing, nevertheless, sufficient humus to retain water and the nutritious elements dissolved in it. There must be enough organic life in the soil; this can be stimulated by adding rotted stable manure or similar organic material. In winter the water level should preferably not be less than 1 m (1 yd) below the surface. The ground should be well draining so that no puddles remain after rain. In the sketch the blotches represent humus and the spots grains of sand.

How can you obtain such average garden soil, starting with the kind of rubbish heap found in the gardens of most newly built houses? To start with, the digging operation described above will give you plenty of opportunity to get rid of unwanted rubbish. If the soil is very sandy (and light in colour) it is advisable to dig in as much peat as possible; even 'black soil' is not always a good thing. The humus should be mixed mainly with the top 30 cm (12 in.) of soil.

When laying out a new garden, as well as when redesigning an existing one, we should also lightly work in some stable manure, if available. This stable manure should be at least a year old, so that it has rotted to some extent. A quantity of $\frac{1}{2}$–1 cu m to every 100 sq m ($\frac{1}{2}$–1 cu yd to every

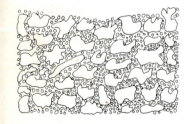

Good soil structure

14

100 sq yd) is sufficient. If farm manure is not available, some good substitutes are spent mushroom compost (but check for lime content before using), leafmould, garden compost, seaweed, or one of the proprietary concentrated organics, such as treated poultry manure or sewage sludge.

If your garden is situated on heavy, firm soil, such as occurs in regions where the soil contains a great deal of loam or clay, you will notice that the surface soon becomes very dense, which prevents water and air penetrating. It is sensible advice to improve such soil with a large quantity of peat, spent hops, etc., which will make it considerably more friable. The best method of incorporating these materials is by rotavating, but you should do this only in dry weather, since otherwise you run the risk that a hard layer will be established, at a depth of 10–20 cm (4–8 in.), which does not let water through. In some places the clay may be so heavy that it can hardly be worked at all. If the garden or the area to be planted is small, you would do best to have all the clay removed mechanically to a depth of 60 cm (24 in.), and replaced by good fibrous loam, which makes gardening very much easier.

Now the plants can go in

After all the operations just described have been completed, you can start planting. Of course you have first made a plan, which will be discussed in more detail in connection with some of the ideas contained in this book. Order your chosen plants in good time from a reliable nurseryman, who can supply a detailed catalogue. There are firms specialising in shrubs, conifers, perennials, water-plants, roses, etc., so there is no need to order them all from one grower.

Deciduous trees, shrubs and hedges are planted in late autumn, when they have lost their leaves. Conifers should be planted a little earlier, from late September to late October, in order to enable them to establish a root system before winter. These plants, as well as evergreen shrubs, are supplied with soil adhering, since the roots should under no circumstances dry out (if rootball appears dry, soak it in water before planting).

Perennials and ornamental grasses can be planted at the same time as conifers, and also in spring, from early March into May, when there is no risk of frost, along with some of the less hardy shrubs such as cistus.

When planting a tree, shrub or conifer in well worked soil,

...ants delivered with soil adhering ...ould first be soaked

15

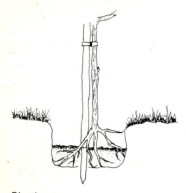

Planting trees

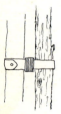

Tree ties

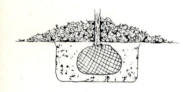

Frost protection

it is sufficient to make a hole large enough to contain the roots spread out to their full length. If the soil at the place of planting is not in good condition, you should make a large hole and mix in rotted farm manure or garden compost with the existing soil some weeks before planting.

Planting is easier if done by two people. While one person holds the tree or shrub upright at the correct depth (note the difference in colour on the stem!), a helper fills in the soil. Move the tree gently up and down, so that the soil gets well in between the roots. Add a few bucketfuls of water, making a nice mud-pool. Finally, fill in the rest of the hole with soil and stamp it down well, using your full weight, then rake the surface lightly, so that it is not compacted.

Trees must be staked to prevent them blowing over in the first few years. The stake is put in to the hole before planting and rammed down thoroughly. Next the tree is planted and tied to the support by means of a plastic tree-band; tree and stake are kept apart by another plastic strap. Tighten the band as much as possible, but do not forget to loosen slightly in subsequent years.

Since, in the case of conifers and evergreens, moisture evaporates even during winter, it is essential to prevent them drying out. This can be achieved by covering the surrounding soil with straw, bracken, or if necessary, fibrous peat. This will also help with frost protection, particularly important with newly planted subjects. Water regularly with some lukewarm water, even in December and January if the soil is very dry.

Perennials will present no problems, since they strike very easily. Plant them straight from the containers in which they are sold. Water plants for small pools are nowadays generally planted in asbestos/cement containers filled with clayey soil. This is a very practical method, as the plants can thus be moved easily.

The smallest pond

Water-lilies cannot grow in a small pool, for they demand deep water. This is an often heard remark, but the photograph shows that it is an untrue one. There are a great many dwarf water-lilies, such as *Nymphaea pygmea* 'Alba' (white) and 'Helvola' (yellow), 'Elitania' (bright red) and 'James Brydon' (see illustration), which can also be cultivated in a larger size. Enquire from a specialist in water-plants. The water need not be more than 20 cm (8 in.) deep, but there should be a 10–15 cm (4–6 in.) deep layer of clay soil.

The photograph further shows arrow-grass *(Sagittaria)*, pickerel weed *(Pontederia)* with blue flowers and mare's tail *(Hippuris)*, which has very fine foliage.

As small pools are easily damaged by frost, it is advisable to cover them in winter with a thick layer of straw or bracken.

A barrel cut across, a concrete bowl — anything may be used to make a small pool. By way of finish I would give preference to coarse grit.

pool made of a bisected barrel

An attractive terrace

In the case of a 'house-in-a-row', the shape of a terrace often creates problems. I therefore give you this example to show how attractive it can be. The photograph and the ground-plan show only part of the garden, which is 6 m (6·5 yd) wide and 15–20 m (16–22 yd) long – in other words, long and narrow. To conceal this effect, the garden designer has created a barrier about halfway down the garden; this consists of the pool, with millstone and pebbles seen in the photograph. The effect is heightened by the simple pergola protecting the terrace. Its construction is very simple: wooden ceiling beams, notched to a third of their thickness on the junctions, and stained dark brown. Climbers may be grown over the entire area, but this is by no means essential, particularly as such plants would rob the house of light.

Another striking feature is the fact that the designer has daringly used ordinary red concrete tiles, 50 × 50 cm (20 × 20 in.). This is a material which is not very popular, but in this case it nevertheless creates a pleasant effect, probably as a result of the contrast provided by the scattered stones and especially by the bluish cobblestones forming the terrace. This lay-out need not cost a great deal. The plan indicates the way in which the terrace is edged by the red tiles. The construction of the foundation for tiles and cobblestones is described in the chapter 'Design your garden'. The fine old millstone in the centre forms the *pièce de résistance* – this is a rare item, difficult to find. If necessary you might get a stonemason to make you one. The central hole has been enlarged slightly, so that it will hold water continuously supplied by a small pump placed underneath. The water runs over the millstone and drips into the small pond. The sketch shows how it works and also the fact that the millstone rests on posts, preferably made of concrete.

The basin in the pebble-bed is easily made by placing a sheet of strong black polythene sheeting in the pit and covering this carefully with pebbles. Red concrete tiles, as well as stones and pebbles, are obtainable from builders' merchants; for the cobblestones you should approach a road construction firm or your local council. A millstone might be obtained by advertising, or from an antique dealer. Small pumps are sold by aquatic plant nurserymen, etc. The plants surrounding the millstone are *Pennisetum alopecuroides* and bamboo *(Arundinaria murieliae)* (far left).

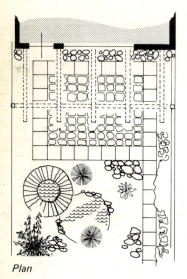

Plan

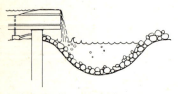

Detail of millstone placing

Ground cover edging garden paths

People who love their gardens but don't want to work in them all day should use far more ground-covering plants. These save a great deal of work, since they discourage weeds. Look at it this way. Nature wishes to cover the earth in order to protect it against burning, dehydration, frost and erosion. If we create a nicely raked piece of ground, *something* will want to grow there, which will then require effort to remove – for plants that grow spontaneously are often no good to us, just weeds: chickweed, couchgrass, nettles, that sort of thing. If, therefore, we plant a garden in such a way that some of the space is necessarily kept bare, we are acting against nature, and in fact, against the rules of good garden maintenance. I'm sorry to have to say this to all those industrious gardeners with their rakes and hoes, but they are going about it the wrong way.

A good garden should not show one square inch of bare soil. Of course this does not apply in the first few years of a newly-constructed garden, when the young plants are still growing, but after a few years the entire area should be covered.

To achieve this effectively we use ground cover, that is annuals and shrubs of creeping habit, which will efficiently spread over the soil. The photograph shows a number of carefully selected specimens along a gracefully sloping path. The chief role is played by *Sedum spurium*, the green plant with the reddish brown buds in the centre of the photograph, which was taken about a month before flowering. By way of contrast it has been interplanted with some clumps of *Festuca glauca*, an easily grown grey-green ornamental grass. The purple flowers covering two low-growing plants are those of *Campanula portenschlagiana* 'Birch Hybrid', which is not a true ground-covering plant but an excellent rock plant. In this particular case it covers stone, which it prefers rather than soil.

To complete the description: in the foreground you see Japanese maple *Acer palmatum* 'Dissectum Ornatum' with its fine red foliage, and in the background the magnificent tall ornamental grass *Miscanthus sacchariflorus*, which may grow to a height of 3 m (8–10 ft). The tree in the background is a sumach.

Ground-covering plants will only be completely successful where soil and situation are perfect. The plants illustrated demand fairly dry, well-drained soil.

Ideal ground-covering plants for shady positions are ferns, *Pachysandra terminalis*, the common ivy, creeping

bugle epimedium spp. and *Vinca minor* (periwinkle). Various mosses are also suitable. For half-shady situations, that is, where the sun shines three to six hours a day, the following might be considered: sweet-scented woodruff, heathers such as calluna and erica in variety, *Cotoneaster dammeri* and other low-growing cotoneasters, hosta, *Juniperus horizontalis*, a low-growing juniper, waldsteinia and most of the plants recommended above for shady positions. In full sun the following are particularly good: *Acaena* or New Zealand burr, especially the species *novae-zelandiae*, cerastium. *Cotoneaster dammeri* and the taller growing *Cotoneaster salicifolius* 'Repens' or 'Parkteppich', *Hypericum calycinum* (St John's wort), *Polygonum affine*, various kinds of sedum and thyme.

Before buying large quantities it is advisable first to try out the various plants. Within a year you will see which plants grow best and only then should you make a definite plan and order the quantities required.

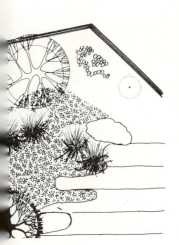

an

A sunken area gives shape to the garden

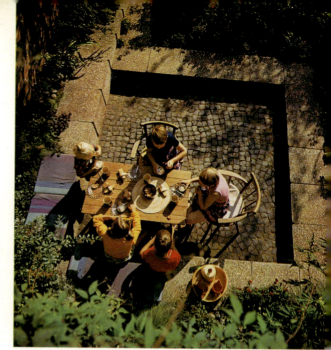

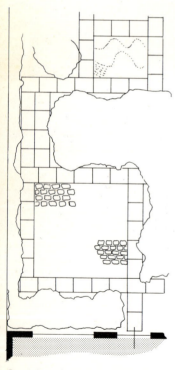

Sandpit at the bottom of the garden

A sunken seating area creates shape and intimacy, as well as improving the garden's perspective — all good reasons for the increasing popularity of this feature. Moreover, the sunken area in the photograph dominates the garden because its edges form the sole pathways. This is an excellent solution where a wide path is not required, and it leaves more space for plants.

The sketch shows a second, smaller, sunken area in the same garden, serving as a sandpit. The division between the two areas consists of fairly tall plants (for instance cotoneaster, together with a small tree, aralia or rhus), which prevents the entire garden being visible at a glance. One might also plant something near the window of the house, for instance some slender grasses.

The edges of the sunken area have been constructed from 50 × 40 × 40 cm (20 × 16 × 16 in.) garden stone.

Further details of similar elements are found on pages 26, 65, 84 and elsewhere. The area itself has been paved with natural stone. Note the different levels of the edges.

he useful trough

At one time feeding troughs were made of sandstone and hewn from one piece. In England sinks were sometimes made of natural stone. All such antique objects may be given a prominent place in the garden (I myself have a pig-feeding trough which is 250 years old).

Troughs may be used in two ways. The first idea is to drill drainage holes in the bottom, which should then be covered with a good layer of drainage material and sandy soil. The trough may thus be used for growing alpine plants. The other idea, illustrated in the photograph, is to fill the trough with water. Because of the danger of frost this is a solution for summer only. In this case one might plant water hyacinth *(Eichhornia)*, usually grown as an annual. Not only does this plant produce beautiful flowers in June—July, it is also very decorative at other times. The flowers next to the trough in the photograph belong to the firethorn *(Pyracantha)*.

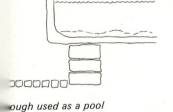

ough used as a pool

An original sandpit

Every child loves a sandpit and no garden where young children play should be without it. But there is no reason why we should not use an attractive variation of the original shape.

This was done by the garden designer Victor von Delius in the long and narrow garden illustrated on p. 36, where you will also find a sketch indicating the position of the sandpit shown in detail on this page. It is situated next to the parent's sitting area, while a play area for older children has been created elsewhere. Small children, after all, like to play safely near their mothers.

And they should *feel* safe in this cosy sandpit, made of heavy pine posts which can incline outwards a little. The centres of tree trunks from which veneer has been shaved may also be used for this purpose. The tops of the posts should be bevelled, so that the child cannot hurt itself.

The construction of such a pit is shown in the sketch. The posts are dug in rather than stamped in, and the bottom is filled with rubble, so that rainwater will soak through. If the level of the ground water should nevertheless prevent this, drainage should be supplied in the form of a drain pipe, if possible connected to the house drainage system.

It is important to have a fairly deep layer of sand, since otherwise the cosy effect of sitting in a pit would be lost. The outer edge of the posts might be surrounded by a layer of heavy plastic or corrugated material to prevent black soil penetrating. The sketch will show that it is not difficult to form a junction between paving and vegetation.

Slightly older children might like the sandpit to be under cover, creating a small hut. A covering is useful also to keep out cats, but this can be achieved equally well with wire netting. Be sure to use the correct sand — river sand will not make sandpies!

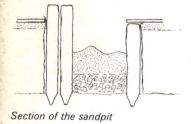

Section of the sandpit

Roses in a pentagon

Roses are among the best garden shrubs, because the flower for such long periods and are relatively easy t maintain. Consequently there are few gardens without a least a few roses. Usually they are planted in a square c circular bed next to a path or a lawn. Since this book intended to give you some unusual ideas, I illustrate a sma rose-garden which I have made at home.

The original idea — and this is shown in the plan — wa inspired by classical rose-gardens, which are often groupe in sections round a statue or a small fountain. Usually th sections are divided by sandy or brick paths and the rose beds are edged with low box hedges. For various reasons did not want to do this. Not only would the design not hav been very original, but I also dreaded the amount of wor created by the little hedges, which have to be trimmed, mak it more difficult to work among the roses, and shade th lower part of the rose-bushes, causing the foliage to die o Another disadvantage of such a small circular garden with statue or a fountain in the middle is, to my mind, the fact tha although it has a centre, there is nothing you can do with I wanted at least to be able to sit there and admire the beau around me. At about the time that I formulated this ide D-shaped concrete elements in 60° curved sections can on the market. Although the inner side is open, they can k supplied closed on request. I dug a circular pit to a depth 10 cm (4 in.) and filled this in with a concrete mortar ba reinforced with wire netting. When the level slab ha hardened, the six elements, which together form a perfe circle, were placed on top. I covered the inside with prim and two coats of glass fibre polyester, thus creating a fir pond.

I had some porphyry stones left over from another job, f paving the paths, but I did not want just to distribute the over the soil, since weeds would have grown among the and the edges would have been trodden down. I therefo drew a large circle on the ground, divided it into five ar drew five paths from the centre to the perimeter. These we dug to a depth of 15 cm (6 in.) and covered with concre mortar. When the concrete had nearly set, a thin layer fresh mortar was spread, into which the stones we pressed. The same treatment was applied around the pon making a circular path wide enough to walk on. Later on t stones were pointed with black cement, but I must adm that this was quite a job.

When the five beds had been dug, the roses were plant

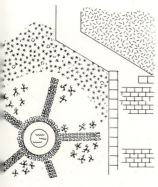

(in spring!); I selected flowers in one shade only, but of course one might plant a variety. To edge the beds I chose purple-blue *Salvia farinacea* 'Blue Bedder', a half-hardy annual which goes very well with roses.

One further hint. Among the very young rose plants (the photograph was taken only four months after planting) you will notice a brown substance: grass clippings taken from the lawn behind the rose-garden. I use the lot for mulching the roses — it is excellent for the soil and saves me an entire year of weeding. You may not think it very attractive, but one soon gets used to it, and once the roses have matured you will hardly see the clippings. Moreover, it helps to retain soil moisture in dry spells.

A wooden fence for privacy

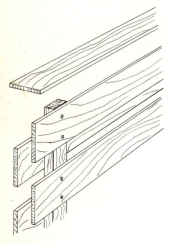

The most generally used wooden fence, with horizontal planking

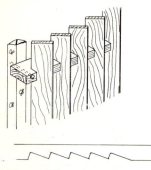

Slats at 45° angle

A garden is really only a 'garden' if it is enclosed. I olden days gardens were enclosed by hedges, and these a still to be recommended because they provide such goo nesting places for the birds. However, in small mode gardens, hedges have proved to take up too much space, an this is the main reason why wooden fences have become s popular. Also much more time has to be spent in keepin them tidy.

The photograph proves that a modern wooden fence considerably more attractive than the hoarding of earli times. As a rule it is constructed in such a way that the wir can pass through. As a result it will not so easily be blow over and it forms a better windbreak than a close-built fenc which may trap the wind. As you know, many fine garde plants depend for their growth on a favourable, modera climate. Especially on new housing estates, where the wir howls round the brick boxes, wind-breaking fences are the greatest importance for protecting in particular tend and newly put-in plants.

The upper sketch shows a type of fencing which is ve popular nowadays. The uprights are of hardwood, 2·7 (9 ft) high. Planed deal boards, 17·5 × 2·5 cm (7 × 1 are attached alternately to the inside and the outside of t uprights. It is up to you how much they overlap. It advisable to use brass screws. (If you prefer to use concre posts, see p. 33.) The horizontal plank on top of the fen serves to divert some of the rainwater.

This fence has the disadvantage that it is easily climbe If you want your fence to be viewproof from one angle on use the design in the second sketch. You start by attachi two firm boards, at top and bottom, to wooden or concre posts. These two planks have angled indentations at regu intervals; they have to be made very carefully, as otherwi the fence will become uneven. The upright slats are the attached by means of screws. A long fence made this w gives an excellent spatial effect.

Finally, there is the wooden fence illustrated in t photograph. In this case the fence is constructed on a base square metal tubing, welded together in places and erect in concrete bases. Take care to treat the tubing with a ru proofer. The wooden sections, extra thick in this case, a best attached by means of screws, as shown in the sket on the left.

A few words about treating the wood. Painting varnishing are out of date, as this repeatedly creates a gre

Wooden fence shown in the photograph

deal of work. Nor do I advise creosoting, which smells unpleasant. Recommended brands of wood-preservers, which will not be harmful to plants, are best. They are easily applied, for instance by dipping the boards, or spraying them, but even a large brush will do the work quickly. A restful, dark brown shade harmonises well with all flower colours; there is also green. Every two or three years the fence should be given a new coat.

A greenhouse in the garden

A greenhouse is simply a delightful glass room in t⬛ garden, and if you can spare about an hour a day for ⬛ pleasant hobby, I strongly advise you to get one. 'As soon ⬛ I close the door of the greenhouse behind me,' a rather ten⬛ businessman told me once, 'I'm in a different world, even ⬛ come straight from the office'. The photograph shows him ⬛ his agreeable work.

One of the questions which might be raised is: what is t⬛ best place for a greenhouse? I have therefore sketched t⬛ plan of a terraced house, about 6–7 m (7–8 yd) wi⬛ (bottom of the sketch), with roughly south-facing garde⬛ You will see the greenhouse in the upper left-hand corn⬛ the arrow indicates the entrance — on the south wall, as ⬛ should be. The greenhouse itself faces north—south, whi⬛ is the most favourable position. A not too large tree (t⬛ may be in your neighbour's garden) throws light shade ⬛ the greenhouse in summer, between 11 and 4 o'clock.

In this example the garden is about 10–12 m (11–13 y⬛ long. Near the house is a sunken area with a pond, su⬛ rounded by flowers and flowering shrubs. A path leads fro⬛ the kitchen door to a narrow hedge, which conceals t⬛ greenhouse as well as a tiny kitchen garden — not lar⬛ enough to feed a family (this requires an area of 400–600 ⬛ m) (480–720 sq yd), but large enough to have some f⬛ with. There is enough room left over for a compost co⬛ tainer and in the greenhouse you can grow young plar⬛ from seed. If, for instance, you become a fuchsia fanatic ⬛ some stage, you can always create a small fuchsia garden ⬛ the back.

If in winter all you want to do is to keep the greenhou⬛ free from frost, a paraffin burner (e.g. an Aladdin) is sufficie⬛ If you wish to maintain a higher temperature, an elect⬛ heater is advisable. Although expensive to run, it is easy ⬛ regulate, which is worth a great deal. The necessary cabl⬛ can easily pass through the flower-bed on the left-hand sic⬛ A light in the greenhouse is useful, especially in winter.

Greenhouses are obtainable in cedarwood and ⬛ aluminium. They can be bought ready-made or in constru⬛ tion kits.

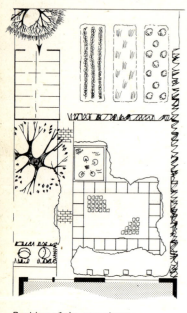

Position of the greenhouse

The least expensive flower garden

The photograph above shows the cheapest way obtain a garden full of flowers. True, it lacks variety and useless for most purposes. But nevertheless it looks deligh ful and it has cost only a few pounds!

This treatment is chiefly advised for a new garden, wh time is lacking in spring to do much in the garden. In th case just level the soil to some extent and get rid of t weeds. Buy a mixture of annual flower seed — sufficient cover the area of your garden. Distribute the seed carefu over the available ground and await results. It will gi pleasure until early in September.

Even established gardens usually have small uncultivat areas, for example under shrubs, along a hedge, near a dri If you sow a mixture of annual flower seed every year, the spots will look a great deal more cheerful. To create original transition between lawn and border, avoiding t ugly sharp edges, you might sow a strip of 50 cm (20 i width with these seeds every year. The grass is cut clos along this strip.

...ving in twill pattern

...nstruction of fence. Left: from side; Right: from above

This is a well-known situation: a fairly busy street passes the one section of your garden where you might relax. What to do in such a case?

It has been found that the best solution is to build a strong wooden fence and to lower the seating area. The photograph shows the result. In extreme cases I would dig even deeper, provided the water table allows this. The sunken area is edged by concrete blocks and paved with bricks in a twill pattern (see sketch).

The wooden fence is of a well-known type. The posts are made of hardwood, 70 cm (28 in.) underground and 200 cm (80 in.) above. Use 17.5×2.5 cm (7×1 in.) deal planks, either planed or cut smoothly. These should be attached to the posts by means of roundheaded brass screws. If you prefer to use concrete posts, use the construction shown on the right in the lower sketch (seen from above). A plank of 4-cm ($1\frac{3}{4}$-in.) thickness is bolted against the post to hold the screws. You could paint the concrete posts dark brown to make them less obvious.

33

A small heather garden

If your taste is for a natural garden, you might consider heather garden. Heathers spread rapidly and form excelle ground cover. Nowadays there is such an enormous choic of richly flowering strains that such a garden might provic colour from January until December, one section aft another. By combining the heathers with conifers and number of carefully chosen flowering shrubs, an attracti whole may be achieved.

The main thing to remember is that practically all heathe flourish only in acid, moisture-retaining soil. *Erica carnea* an exception as it will tolerate lime but not chalky, shallo soil. Clay soil is definitely unsuitable, but peaty or sandy s will give good results. If the soil is too dry, it should mixed before planting with a large quantity of peat in son form or other, as well as with some well-rotted stab manure. Light shade, provided by a few trees such birches, is best, to prevent the plants drying out too much summer; spraying with tapwater, which is often ratf chalky, is not much good in a drought.

A heather garden usually contains few architectu features, but there is no reason why you should not co struct a terrace or a path, for instance by using railw sleepers. It would also be quite attractive to comb heathers with very modern materials, but this is rarely do

The following are a few suggestions for the year in t heather garden. January is the time for the winter-floweri *Erica carnea*. Strains such as 'Praecox Rubra' (pale purpl red), 'Snow Queen' (white) and 'Winter Beauty' (de purple pink) may flower until late March. *E.* x *darleyen* which is somewhat sensitive to frost, flowers in the sa period, for instance the pure white 'Silberschmelze'. La flowering *Erica carnea* (March-April) cultivars are, amo others, 'James Backhouse' (purple-pink) and 'Vive (purplish-red). May is a little difficult, but a white *E darleyensis* may still be in flower and if you are willing provide some protection, *E. mediterranea* 'W.T. Rack (pure white) can be very beautiful.

June once more brings plenty of flowers, for it is now t the native *E. cinerea* appears with strains such as 'C Eason' (magenta red), 'Pallas' (purple) and 'Alba Min (white). Some strains of the native cross-leaved er *E. tetralix*, are beginning to flower now, for instance 'A (white) and 'Ken Underwood' (carmine-pink). Even strain of the ling heather *Calluna vulgaris* is coming i flower at this time, namely 'Tib' (pure purple).

During July, August and September we have a tremendous choice of strains of *E. cinerea, E. tetralix, C. vulgaris* and *E. vagans* — too numerous to mention. *E. vagans* 'Rubra' continues to flower well into October, as do some of the *C. vulgaris* races such as 'Alba Plena' (white), 'David Eason' (purple), and 'Goldsworth Crimson' (carmine red). Some strains, moreover, have colourful winter foliage, for instance 'Cuprea', 'Gold Haze', 'Multicolour', 'Robert Chapman', 'Serlei Aurea' and 'Winter Chocolate'. In the course of November the earliest strains of *E. carnea*, such as 'Praecox Rubra', start to flower again.

In order to keep your heathers compact and free-flowering, it is essential to cut them back thoroughly immediately after flowering, at least every two years. This is a substitute for their being eaten by sheep, as happens on the moors.

Occasionally some peat should be scattered among the plants, as well as some well-rotted cow manure.

The narrow garden

This little book deals mainly with sections of garden
nevertheless I should like to show you a number of solution
for an entire garden. The one illustrated is a good example o
a long and narrow one. It is only 6 m (6½ yd) wide – th
house is one of a terrace – and at least 20 m (22 yd) lon
No matter if yours is a few metres longer or shorter: the ma
thing is the way in which the German garden designer Vict
von Delius has dealt with the 12 m (13 yd) nearest the hous

The sketch below (but not the photograph) shows that
narrow terrace about 1½ m (1½ yd) wide, has been con
structed next to the house. This is useful for getting in an
out of the house, for washing the windows, and so on. It
not suitable for sitting on, for in this particular case it is to
much in the shade of the house. Hence the second terrac
halfway down the garden. It might equally well be sited
the bottom of the garden. The link between the tw
terraces is well thought out; it consists of concrete til
which appear to float in a sea of pebbles, creating a clea
bridging effect.

The spatial impact is strengthened by the use of U-shape
concrete elements, seen to the right of the path and arou
the sitting area. Further details of these useful elements will
found on pages 65 and 84. You will note that the 60 × 40 c
(24 × 16 in.) washed concrete tiles are linked by reddi
brown strips. These consist of building bricks, laid flat. V
Delius of course placed these bricks across the path, one
the tricks used to minimise the narrow effect of the garde
Another, even better, trick is the way this garden has be
divided into a number of square sections. Once the plan
have matured it will be impossible for the entire garden to
seen from the living room; hidden places have been create
which give a scenic effect and improve the perspective.

To the left of the terrace you will see an original sandp
constructed of thick, short posts. Details are shown in t
photograph on p. 25. Young children can play happily he
near their parents. For older children there is plenty of roc
at the bottom of the garden. This area can be optica
separated from the terrace by planting a hedge or a row
tall grasses across the garden.

This is a garden which you can easily lay out yourse
Slabs and concrete sections are simple to place into positi
and very little soil needs to be moved. Vegetation, ve
varied in the garden illustrated, may be entirely differe
Details of this garden are to be found on pages 24 and 6

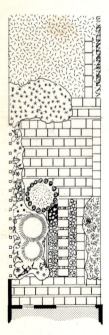

Plan of the narrow garden

A path plus something extra

What you see in the photograph is merely a small section of a garden, a simple corner which might be found anywhere. It is not expensive or difficult to make, but it has atmosphere because it has been created with love.

On the left you can see a small part of the lawn, which terminates in three layers of railway sleepers. They are particularly fine sleepers, bound with iron to prevent them splitting. The path, constructed of circular washed concrete tiles, lies on a lower level, approximately 30 cm (12 in) below. I don't know why round tiles are used so rarely, for the illustration shows that they are very attractive.

They may be obtainable from a well-stocked garden centre or builders' merchant; if not, you might be able to have them made by one of the many small establishments which do this sort of thing. By the way, you might also consider very large circular slabs, 80–100 cm (34–40 in) across. These can be used in all sorts of attractive ways.

When circular tiles are used to make a path, large pebbles are ideal for filling in the spaces, as has been done in this case. The base consists of a layer of rubble (for drainage) which prevents the soil from working itself upwards. A corner like this should not be created in a low-lying place, for the rocky character would thus be lost.

Vegetation is somewhat wild, to give the garden a natural aspect. It contains several cotoneasters, and all kinds of rock plants might be placed among the stones, provided they tolerate some shade. In my experience many plants which winter rot in an ordinary garden bed will survive among tiles. The roots withdraw to the relatively dry soil underneath the stone, where they obviously feel better. Moreover, concrete tiles release some chalk, which plants are able to absorb.

If you would like to extend the idea, I could recommend a small terrace on the right-hand side. This might, for example, be made of railway sleepers, perhaps with a small pond, as shown on p. 17. Restrict yourself to tranquil looking plants and do not use too many colours.

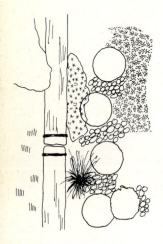

The path seen from above

A moat around the house

Garden architecture frequently uses symbolic motifs: th pergola and the sunken area for protection, safety; the soun of water for tranquillity. On the facing page you see a symbo of isolation: the moat. It might indicate the desire of recluse, who wants to shut himself inside his house, awa from everyday life, but it might also symbolise someone' undeniable need to raise the bridge when he sees hi mother-in-law approach. For a bridge is included, complet with raising mechanism.

It is the idea of the German garden designer Richar Bödeker, who constructed the moat round the former railwa station at Neanderthal, where he lives. Apart from the advantages already mentioned, I could suggest a few others The house, which in this case could do with some extr features, has been separated from the garden in an interestin manner. In Amsterdam and Venice, as well as in the case o ancient castles, we observe that a house rising from wate always looks distinguished. The photograph proves that t achieve this the moat need not be very wide.

In the second place it is interesting to be able, from one' living room, to watch the delightful movements of goldfisl swimming in groups just below the water surface.

One might ask whether such an effect is hard to achieve This is not as difficult as it might seem. The moat is onl 30–50 cm (12–20 in.) deep; here and there one might dig little deeper to provide a place where fish can spend th winter. In any case the warmth exuded by the house wi prevent an ice layer ever becoming very thick. The bottom o the moat need therefore never come below the foundation of the house, which are usually 70–80 cm (28–32 in.) deep

A 10–15-cm (4–6-in.) thick floor of reinforced concret is laid next to the foundations. At the required distance fror the house (2–3 m; 2–3 yd) a small wall is constructed at th same time. If you use the right kind of mortar, a 15-cr (6-in.) wall can be watertight. The other wall is formed b the foundations of the house, made watertight by severa layers of a combination of polyester and fibreglass. Th polyester should be joined to the new concrete floor by 50-cm (20-in.) overlap, combined with a concrete adhesive I believe this is a better system than constructing a concret wall against the foundations, which takes a lot of time an may easily result in cracks.

If you are having a new house built, with a concret foundation, it is not expensive to have the moat constructe at the same time. Remember that a concrete pond require

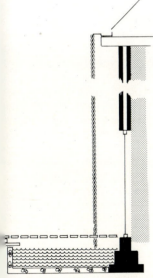

ction of moat, house, bridge and ain

an expansion seam every 3 m (3 yd). This consists of a rubber profile joint which enables the concrete sections to move slightly. If you omit these seams, you will inevitably have cracks later on.

It is also possible to make the entire moat of extra heavy rubber, in which case the seams must be welded. However, it is not easy to achieve a completely watertight result in this manner.

The moat is edged with concrete tiles set in mortar. An interesting detail is the chain which hangs from the gutter and replaces a rainpipe. Even if the chain does not hang straight down, the water will always trickle along the links. The water plants are growing in separate bowls; the water-lily is a variety which will flower freely even in shallow water. Finally a good tip: to prevent damage to the foundations, make sure that the pond never entirely freezes over. The best method is to run a few small pumps during frosty weather.

41

Upright sleepers

The use of railway sleepers in gardens has become quit prevalent — almost too much so. The famous Dutch garde designer Mien Ruys, who started this years ago, can neve have dreamed that there would one day be a shortage of th material, simply because so many people followed h example.

Oddly enough, sleepers are nearly always used horizon tally, as steps, to form seats, etc., and are rarely place upright. The facing photograph of an intimate seating are designed by Wolfgang Miller, however, proves what goo results may be achieved in this manner. The method c placing the sleepers upright is shown in the sketch.

These sleepers are about 2·60 m (8 ft 6 in.) in lengt Begin by sorting them into different lengths and dig narrow groove (the width of a spade) to the depth of sleeper minus 200 or 190 cm (80 or 76 in.). If you wish make a wall 2 m (2 yd) high, you will have to dig to 70 c (28 in.) for 2·70 m (9 ft) sleepers. By using sleepers equal length you will avoid having to adjust each on Carefully ram down the soil at the bottom of the groove the right depth. Two people will now be able to erect tr sleepers quite easily and speedily. Railway sleepers a always thoroughly impregnated and will probably last for further twenty to thirty years. Take care to use only fir choice sleepers; if they are warped they are unsuitable f this purpose.

Dig a groove to the correct depth

It is also quite easy to construct a workshop, a show cabin or a sauna from railway sleepers. The heavy beams a erected in the same way as described above, but this tir in the form of a square. Inside they are linked by strong sla 5–10 cm (2–4 in.) below the top; these support the ro structure, which may slope slightly. The roof is covered wi roofing felt or similar material. Drainage is supplied by 5-cm (2-in.) pvc pipe fitted inside. The door opening formed by omitting two or three sleepers. It is also possik to make a labyrinth entrance. The outside wall is finishe with 30-cm (12-in.) wide deal board, stained with da brown wood preserver. This looks extremely attracti particularly if the board stands out about 5 cm (2½ in.) frc the sleepers. Use spacers or washers for this purpose. Th covering frame, which extends about 5–8 cm (1–3 i above the top of the sleepers, hides possible differences height, as well as imperfections in the finish of the roof. you want the structure to be windproof, you can finish t inside with waterproof hardboard or a similar materi

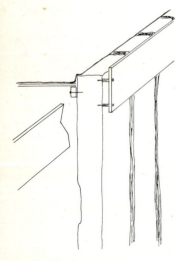

Roof finish of the sauna

...tion of a daybed

Ceiling height can be 200–210 cm (80–84 in.). The sleepers need not be dug in deeper than 40 cm (16 in.), especially if they are firmly linked (metal strip inside).

A few words about the day beds shown in the photograph. These were also made by an amateur, with the aid of a small electric welding apparatus. They consist of square metal tubing, covered with impregnated deal slats. Extremely simple, but most attractive. For the sake of extra comfort you can cover them with thin foam rubber mattresses and cushions.

A patio that has everything

Here is another of those patios in which the entire famil[ ] may feel at home: a room out of doors which has everything such as Victor von Delius, the garden architect, designs s[ ] well. If you like the idea, but think it is somewhat lacking i[ ] greenery, you should bear in mind that all the plants in th[ ] photograph are only in their first growing season. In a fe[ ] years' time the larch, the rhododendrons, azaleas, wistar[ ] and other plants will make this garden look very different.

One of this patio's strong points is undoubtedly the poc[ ] at present a rather uninteresting bit of water with too fe[ ] plants. Long and narrow, canal-shaped ponds are ofte[ ] very effective, probably because natural water (a brook or ditch) is of a similar shape. Of course the water has bee[ ] bridged, and if you look closely, you will see that the grav[ ] slabs continue across the paving, thus linking the two par[ ] of the garden.

The red cushions are placed on a seat made of U-shape[ ] concrete sections. Chairs can be placed on the paving ar[ ] people who prefer the shade can sit in the corner shown tc left in the photograph.

This garden cannot be constructed very cheaply, since t[ ] patio floor as well as the pool are constructed from rei[ ] forced concrete, which need not be made in one section. is, however, essential to build the pond very solidly, prefe[ ] ably with a seam to allow for expansion. The paving ston[ ] are embedded in the concrete and require no maintenanc[ ] Concrete elements are placed on the farthest section of t[ ] base plate, and beyond these is a galvanised square tu[ ] bearing the pergola. Some oddments are seen in the cent[ ] back of the photograph, including pergola beams, met[ ] uprights and a chain which serves to direct rainwater fro[ ] the roof into the pond.

The steps across the water rest on concrete blocks U-shaped elements. Lights have been installed all over t[ ] garden, so that the patio is very suitable for a garden par[ ] As the garden is so sheltered, all the plants will gro[ ] exceptionally well.

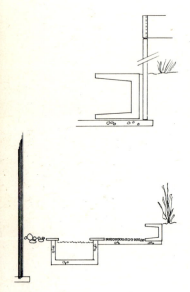

Section of frontage, pond, seating (lower sketch)
Detail of seat and pergola construction (upper sketch)

A garden full of stones

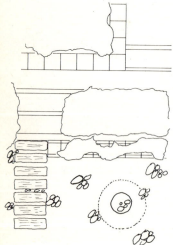

Plan of the garden

The old-fashioned rock garden, a sort of embankment o[ ]which rocks were arranged in a 'natural' manner with alpin[e]plants between, has fortunately gone out of fashion. It was [a]very artificial arrangement. Perhaps it will be replaced by [a]stone garden as shown in the photograph. This is like [a]glacier-bed in which all kinds of plants and garden orna[ ]ments may find a place. In a country like ours this may not b[e]a very natural arrangement either, but it looks very effectiv[e]and is easy to maintain.

The pond, for instance, may be formed by sinking [a]concrete dish or heavy plastic sheeting covered with stone[s.]A small pump placed below the millstone makes the wate[r]circulate. A pathway constructed of railway sleeper[s]bridges the sea of stones — a good idea, this. Differences [of]level are contained by means of concrete elements.

Garden architect: Victor von Delius.

Nothing is more boring in a garden than plants which are all of the same height, or which change from low to tall in an unnaturally gradual manner. In nature a sharp contrast between high and low, between creeping and tall vegetation, is quite normal. If you follow this principle in planting your garden, you will notice a tremendous improvement in its dynamics and sense of space.

The photograph shows an excellent example of this principle. The ground is covered with the creeping *Sedum kamtschaticum*, from which a group of *Miscanthus sinensis* emerges. Personally I like to use the indefatigable *Cotoneaster dammeri*, which forms strong ground cover from which all sorts of plants stand out. *Vinca minor*, or periwinkle, is also useful for ground cover, although less flat-growing. *Empetrum nigrum* (crowberry) is excellent in acid soil in combination with conifers, etc. All kinds of bulbs may be naturalised among ground cover.

Is the border finished?

We always refer to the 'border' when talking about the be
next to a terrace or lawn, but in many cases this is not a tru
border at all, simply a collection of various shrubs an
perennials, with bare patches in between.

The photograph shows what a real border is like. It wa
invented by Gertrude Jekyll, the garden designer who, ear
in the present century, studied the flowering verges alor
country roads and decided that something similar ought to b
possible in the garden. The original border, therefore, cor
sists almost entirely of perennials, selected for their colou
height and flowering period. This is more easily said tha
done, and truly fine borders are nowadays rarely found.

Nevertheless I believe that it is not an impossible task t
create and maintain a beautiful border. If, on seeing th
photograph on the facing page, you agree with me th
such an attractive and fascinating section of the garde
would be worth having, you should bear in mind that th
photograph was taken in the garden of ordinary, thouc
enthusiastic, garden lovers.

A border such as we are now discussing usually consis
of a rectangle of, say, 4×20 m (4×22 yd). A smaller area i
of course, possible, but a depth of at least 3 m (9 ft)
essential. There are also circular, curving and doubl
edged borders. From the front the height of the plants ris
at an angle of about $45°$, because otherwise the flowers
the back would be invisible. It is perfectly feasible to use
number of less dense plants, provided the whole remair
clear.

Although one might strive for a border which flowers f
a maximum period, the best borders are nevertheless tho
which are in full flower for only about six weeks – arour
mid-July. Naturally a June, August or September bord
may be created as well. The main thing is that approximate
three-quarters of the plants should flower simultaneousl
as is the case here.

Next, colour. Personally I always prefer borders which a
not too gaudy. The one illustrated is just possible – mo
colours would create a restless effect. Beautiful combina
tions are: red, lilac, soft yellow (as here); blue and purp
combined with grey; dark red with orange and pale yello
(very difficult to achieve, this!), and rose-pink with viol
and grey. Since you are not a garden designer, you would c
best to create a border over a number of years. You start wi
a basic plan and plant accordingly. During the flowerin
period you write down which plants look well and which a

disappointing, and in due course introduce the necessary changes. In this way the border will improve from year to year. Take care to stake the tall plants carefully when they are in flower, or start to support them with twigs as early as May. Leave everything *in situ* in the autumn and do not remove old foliage *until spring*. Do not dig between the plants — to discourage weeds cover the ground in May with grass cuttings. They will disappear completely.

In the border illustrated, the magnificent lilac clumps are *Campanula lactiflora*, interspersed with fine blue delphiniums. The red colour is provided by a small-flowered floribunda rose, e.g. 'City of Belfast'. The soft yellow plant is Lady's mantle *(Alchemilla mollis)* and in front you see saponaria. Here and there a few blood-red, small-flowered dahlias have been introduced, as well as red and yellow antirrhinums. Start with the four or five main species; the rest will follow automatically.

Garden games

The garden provides many opportunities for play addition to the use of sandpit and swing – and this applie especially to older people. These opportunities are rare exploited – all the more reason to give you a few ideas.

Since for many games the lawn is used, it is importa that this should be firm and level. This means that, before t grass is sown, the soil should be well trodden to close the spaces; it should then be raked level. Sow with a 'gam mixture', consisting of meadow grass and rye grass, wi possibly some creeping red fescue. Such a lawn shou never be mown shorter than 4 cm ($1\frac{3}{4}$ in.); it should regularly fertilised and every two months should be aerate for, as it gets trodden on a great deal, the surface w rapidly become too hard, which may encourage moss.

A typical game for a not too small lawn is croquet. Th game definitely requires a level lawn. If the space available too small for croquet, one might play hoopla instead, illustrated in the photograph on the facing page, actua taken on a roof garden. The game of boulle which in Fran is often played under the plane trees, is best confined to special bowling alley, which need not be of exact propo tions. The section sketched shows how the alley has bee built up from a layer of rubble and a layer of fine grave Spraying and rolling will create a good level surface. wooden frame ensures that the balls will rebound properl

An open-air game of draughts or chess is pleasant on warm summer's day. The board should be constructed in sheltered and slightly shaded spot. The players sit comfortable chairs on the terrace and the board itself consis of sixty-four tiles in two contrasting colours. If you do n have much room, a smaller board can be constructed mosaic on a concrete foundation.

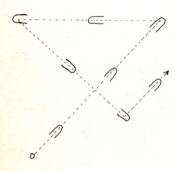

Possible lay-out of croquet lawn

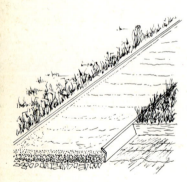

Alley for jeu de boulles

A cosy barbecue pit

Cooking in the open air has become a popular pastime a it is therefore not at all a bad idea to allot a special place the garden for the purpose.

In the garden of a fairly wide semi-detached house, t barbecue was placed in the centre of a circular sunken are This has the obvious advantage that the edge, covered w cushions, will provide seating for quite a number of peop The edge consists of washed concrete elements, holle inside, so that it is possible to lift them. The barbecue its can be made by an amateur, but excellent concrete ones c be bought ready-made. The area has been paved wi natural cobbles and house bricks, used level, have be employed for the terrace. The striking pond at higher le has been constructed from two concrete rings of differe diameter. One of them has been dug in, given a concre floor and filled with gravel. The second, smaller, ring — washed concrete — has also been closed at the bottom a has been placed perfectly level on the gravel. A sm pump, concealed under the second ring, circulates t water, which splashes down gently.

An aralia, still immature, has been planted behind t pond, with in front a clump of pampas grass (Cortaderi also still very young.

Have a look at the interesting wooden fence, whi provides privacy. It has been constructed from holle square metal uprights, set in concrete, as described page 29. A 5-cm (2-in.) space has been left at the botto so that the boards can drain properly. The fence has be stained with a special wood preserver.

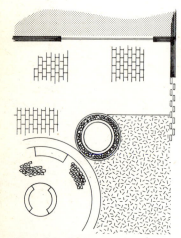

Plan of the barbecue

The roof garden

Now that space at ground level is becoming increasin[...] at a premium, it is time to give more consideration to r[...] gardens. Roofs of apartment buildings, parking garages, [...] provide an enormous amount of space which could be m[...] suitable for vegetation at little cost.

A roof garden weighs 350–700 kg (770–1540 lb) per [...] m (sq yd) (i.e. about 7–14 cwt) and obviously the build[...] must be sufficiently strong to bear this weight. When [...] doubt you would do best to consult an architect or anot[...] building expert. The above figures, however, apply wh[...] the entire roof is covered with a 40 cm (16 in.) layer of s[...] of which 50% is artificial material, or consists of peat s[...] This provides sufficient depth for practically all plants; tre[...] however, must be anchored to prevent them blowing ov[...] The cultivated layer is laid on drainage plates, to prev[...] excess water collecting. Of course the roof must slope v[...] slightly. In summer it will often be necessary to use the ho[...]

In the roof garden shown in the photograph this form [...] construction was impossible, since the roof was not stro[...] enough. This may be your problem as well. In the case il[...] strated the roof has to bear only the washed concr[...] slabs, weighing about 100 kg (220 lb, nearly 2 cwt) per [...] m (sq yd); if this is still too heavy, the terrace may [...] constructed of wood (see page 68). The plants are plac[...] along the edges of the roof and usually rest on the wa[...] which can bear much heavier weights. Even at some distan[...] from the walls a great deal is possible.

In some cases the wall might be extended upwar[...] creating a parapet. If you place a number of concrete bloc[...] at a distance of 60–80 cm (24–32 in.) from this parap[...] flowers may be planted in between.

An easier and cheaper method is to erect two walls [...] concrete slabs, connected by rods. These may be availab[...] ready-made. The elements shown on pages 44 and 65 a[...] also very suitable. Placed upside down, these elemen[...] provide a planting depth of 30–35 cm (12–14 in.). By joini[...] two placed on their sides you gain a depth of 40–45 c[...] (16–18 in.). These sections weigh about 85 kg (187 lb) [...] it is important to check that they can be transported to t[...] roof via the lift or some other means. They may also [...] used on a balcony.

To ensure drainage there should be holes or gaps in t[...] base of the elements. A piece of drainage material in t[...] base is also advisable.

The photograph shows how annuals, perennials a[...]

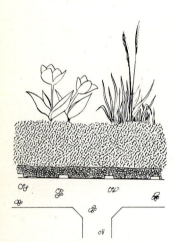

Section of the growing layer

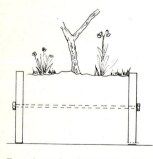

Trough made of concrete slabs

54

*...lanting trough made of a
...-shaped concrete element*

*...ong trough constructed from
...ree elements*

shrubs may all be used in such planting strips. In places where there is a great deal of wind you should restrict yourself to strong plants and trees, which will grow anywhere, for instance poplars, willows, birches, rowan trees, Austrian pines, privet, cotoneaster, sea buckthorn, etc., and you should use many biennials, such as the Yellow Mullein *(Verbascum)* shown here.

The pergola is important to create a sense of intimacy in the sitting area. A vine would look well on this, for instance the easily fruiting 'Brant'.

A nice wild garden

I'd rather have a wild garden, some people say nowadays, better than all that artificial business. But they do not know how to achieve such a garden, nor what the consequences will be. Hence this short essay.

It is almost impossible to make a truly wild garden, since this should in fact contain only flowers which would grow there naturally. A garden that has been allowed to grow wild or a garden with a wild character, is a different matter. In this case we choose strong, non-cultivated plants, without much regard to their native habitat. We may also collect seeds of native and exotic flora and scatter them in the garden. Plants that want to grow there will perpetuate themselves.

If a piece of virgin land is to be turned into a 'wild' garden it is advisable, nevertheless, to plan it to some extent. I take it that you want to be able to move in the garden without trampling on the plants. This means that there must be paths, and stone or concrete paths at that, since otherwise they would be overgrown. You may also like to be able to sit or sunbathe somewhere and this means that you must construct a terrace in a suitable spot. This should preferably be made of a natural material, but should of course also be hard. Needless to say a lawn is not a practical proposition and if children and dogs play in the garden you may take it for granted that the natural design will come to nothing. Walking outside the hardened sections should be avoided as much as possible, for this will spoil the structure of the soil and since there is something growing everywhere, plants are bound to get trodden on.

A very useful device in the creation of varying environments for growth is the construction of different levels which result in drier and damper areas in the garden. Louis le Roy, who might be said to have introduced the 'wild' garden to the Netherlands, has solved the problem by building dry stone walls in different parts of his garden. These vary in height between 10 and 50 cm (4 and 20 in.) and consist of old bricks, preferably from demolished buildings, to which lime adheres. A dry stone wall is made by stacking the bricks without mortar. Usually such a wall serves to contain the soil; in that case it should slope slightly (see sketch). In Mr le Roy's garden the paths consist of natural flagstones, all edged by these little walls. Here and there he has used larger fragments to create dry hills. He believes that the lime released in this manner benefits the growth of all plants. The thousands of slugs living among the stone eat the algae off the trees, with the

Plan of a wild garden

result that his trees appear polished. Dry stone walls are marvellous for planting; this was realised as much as fifty years ago.

Of course a wild garden is never dug; dead leaves are not removed; fallen branches and twigs are broken up and thrown among the plants. No fertiliser is ever used. Unwanted plants, such as weeds, may be removed, but Mr le Roy does not even do that. In fact he only maintains the paths.

In the course of the years a wild garden will grow constantly denser and darker, which results in a change of vegetation. If you find that everything grows bare for lack of light, you cut down a tree and leave it where it falls. Don't forget to observe the fascinating way in which nature makes things grow unexpectedly in the strangest places.

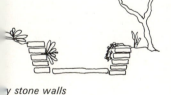

y stone walls

A water patio

Why should a garden always consist of land with at mo[st]
a little water? Why not reverse the situation? This wa[s]
probably the reasoning of the garden designer George
Boesch, who designed the garden illustrated on the facin[g]
page for a childless couple born under the sign of Pisces.

Doubtless a glacier was his inspiration, for in the centre [of]
the photograph one sees clearly that the stones appear [to]
roll down into the water, as if a giant hand had scattere[d]
them in the patio. The sparse planting of fir trees visible i[n]
the foreground, heightens the impression of a mounta[in]
landscape.

If you should decide to make such a water garden, yo[u]
should, of course, be aware of the consequences. To beg[in]
with a watertight basin has to be constructed; this is be[st]
done while the bungalow (house) is being built. If th[e]
foundations are of concrete, the basin can be laid at the sam[e]
time. This has not been done in the case of the garde[n]
illustrated, as may be seen from the lighter-coloured ri[m]
between the pond and the wall of the house. Obviously th[e]
house had already been built when the idea of a wat[er]
garden was born. A new frame was therefore made, th[e]
reinforcement installed, and a concrete basin constructe[d.]
One side of the framework was obviously formed by th[e]
existing foundation. The centre, where the water-li[ly]
grows, is on a lower level; the depth here is about 70 c[m]
(28 in.). The rest of the pond need not be deeper tha[n]
30–40 cm (12–16 in.). The pebbles on the bottom will in an[y]
case create an impression of depth.

A striking feature are the circular stepping stones whic[h]
enable one to move about in the garden. These circul[ar]
blocks can be bought ready-made and can be placed on th[e]
bottom of the pool; it is also possible to construct them at th[e]
same time as the bottom, before the concrete has set. [In]
this case a piece of plastic tubing may be used as a moul[d.]

Such a water garden has a strongly reflective effec[t]
making the interior of the house much lighter. It is therefo[re]
an excellent solution for small, closed-in patios which do n[ot]
receive much sunlight. You will moreover tan twice [as]
quickly when you are sunbathing. For this purpose a sma[ll]
'floating' terrace might be incorporated, large enough for tw[o]
deck chairs. Madam may ask how the windows are to b[e]
cleaned. Well, either you engage someone with a talent f[or]
balancing acts, who can keep his or her equilibrium on th[e]
stepping stones, or you get some good waterproof boots an[d]
get into the water. Every problem has its solution!

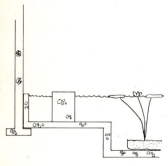

*Section of pond with stepping
stones*

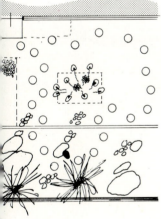

The ordinary plants grow in concrete boxes, which may be placed anywhere on the bottom of the pool. Fill them with clay soil. The larger part of the soil dug out to make the pond has been used in the front part of the patio, which slopes fairly steeply. This bank was covered in rubble, after which the large stones were put into place. The great contrast in levels makes the patio appear much larger, and it is moreover economical to use the soil.

The stones can be bought from specialist firms. If the patio is completely walled in it will be necessary to use a crane to place them.

A garden for the children

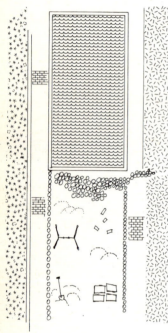

Plan of children's play area and swimming pool

The garden belongs to the whole family, including the children, but a beautifully designed garden does not take kindly to children's games. Just think what will happen to your fine lawn if it is trodden on in winter, or to the border composed with such care (for instance the one on page 49 if a football lands in it at frequent intervals. It just won't do

To my mind the best solution for this problem is a carefully designed garden where a separate area has been reserved for the children. For instance, you may have a long, narrow strip of ground, like the garden on page 37. An attractive solution is to make a partition halfway down the garden behind which the children can play to their heart's content You can relax on the terrace while the young can make as much mess as they like and don't even have to clear it up afterwards.

This solution has purposely not been chosen for the fairly large garden illustrated opposite. Here the children occupy the centre of the garden, where an enormous sandpit forms a striking element of the design. It is entirely surrounded by circular posts of varying heights, so that the children's domain is clearly defined. True, you can't play football here either, but no garden is suitable for such games.

On the left of the photograph you can see a small section of the border, which here forms a fairly steep bank contained by a concrete edge which at the same time encloses the path. This is a good idea, for without such an edge the soil would constantly spill over on to the path. To the right and behind the climbing posts the path ends in a small lawn A small section of the swimming-pool, 4 × 8 m (4 × 9 yd), is just visible behind the partition. The sketch shows the lay out. A sitting area might be created beyond the pool.

It is logical to situate the swimming-pool and the children's play area in the sunniest part of the garden. The design is truly original. I believe that a similar one could successfully be adapted to a garden of at least 500 sq m (500 sq yd).

Contrasting shape and colour

In planting our garden we should always strive to achiev
both contrast and harmony in shape and colour. This is muc
more easily said than done. Contrast in shape is achieved by
for example, growing a clump of slender grass among groun
cover consisting of creeping plants such as *Stipa pennata* c
Cotoneaster dammeri. Contrast can also be created b
growing large or composite flowers among plants wit
insignificant flowers. In the example illustrated on th
facing page, a yellow lily has been placed next to gypsophila
while a slightly deeper yellow kniphofia provides an equall
striking contrast.

Who said that white and yellow do not go together? It i
simply a matter of using the right shade of yellow, which i
this case means a slightly lemony shade. Moreover, th
combination should not be spoiled by the introduction o
further colours. It is best to leave it at this.

Another golden rule is that plants should be used i
groups of varying size. In the example illustrated dozens o
yellow lilies would spoil the effect.

Gypsophila of course does not flower all through th
summer. It is for that reason that a clump of irises has bee
incorporated; these have now finished flowering, but th
shape of the foliage provides a fine contrast. No doubt othe
plants provided the colour contrast during the flowerin
period of the irises, for instance rock rose *(Helianthemun*
hybrids), heuchera, or globe-flowers *(Trollius).* Backgroun
plants such as Michaelmas daisies, *Aconitum* x *arends*
(monk's hood), *Helianthus decapetalus* (a small type o
sunflower) and autumn-flowering anemone hybrids ar
obvious choices for when the gypsophila has cease
flowering.

Such a design is best achieved with the aid of a table, i
which colour, height, flowering period and growing condi
tions of about a hundred different perennials have bee
systematically arranged. Look out for gardening books whic
contain such tables.

Hide the dustbin

It is always such a pity when a beautifully design garden is spoiled by the dustbins or refuse-bags near t kitchen door. Alas, we cannot do without them.

The problem could be solved by constructing a sm open storage space. In the photograph the dustbin hidden by the cotoneaster.

The sketch shows six further solutions. Above left, special concrete box with a metal door with refuse-b holder. This box is fairly expensive, but it is a very so affair.

Above right is a paling fence, with an alcove attache Centre left a hedge and centre right a fence made of uprig railway sleepers, with alcove attached. Lower left, wooden fence with a low partition in the same style. Low right, a brick wall.

One might think of at least six other solutions. The m thing is that you should *do* something about it.

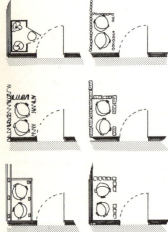

Six hiding places

sing concrete
ections

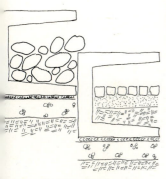

ncrete elements forming steps

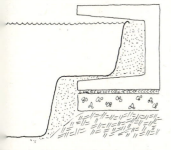

thod of incorporating the pool

U-shaped concrete sections, also known as D-elements, etc., are ideal for creating variations in level. The photograph shows a garden which I designed for someone in Breukelen and the sketches the ease of construction.

The upper sketch shows a section of the step in the foreground. The sections have been mounted in a 8–10-cm (5–6-in.) unreinforced concrete layer, laid between two planks and then levelled. When it has set, add a 2-cm ($\frac{3}{4}$-in.) layer of mortar and position the elements in this. They weigh about 85 kg (187 lb) each.

The lower sketch shows the incorporation of a fibreglass pool, which is visible in the photograph as well. Here the most difficult operation is the filling in with sand, which must be done carefully since otherwise the pool will bulge.

These concrete sections are supplied in a size of 45 × 45 × 45 cm (18 × 18 × 18 in.). The pavement consists of 10 × 10 × 10 cm (4 × 4 × 4 in.) black concrete bricks.

The garden at night

Many owners of beautiful gardens are out all day and a[re] able to enjoy their private bit of nature only in the eveni[ngs] and at weekends. If the sitting-room window gives a go[od] view of the garden, a few small outside lights will enable y[ou] to spend several pleasant evening hours looking out at t[he] flowers. It will also form an attractive and colourful bac[k]ground when you are having drinks with friends, either [in] or out of doors.

In view of all these advantages I am constantly surpris[ed] that so little use is made of light in the garden, even [by] garden designers. When the garden is being constructed it [is] easy and inexpensive to bury an electric cable, which m[ay] be quite difficult later on. Once the cable has been installe[d] lights can be added at a later stage.

I like to make a distinction between *light* and *illuminati[on]* in the garden. *Light* implies a number of garden lamps, whi[ch] ensure that you don't break your neck at night — in oth[er] words, a light to guide you. *Illumination*, on the other han[d] means that the entire garden is floodlit.

There is no reason why we should not do both; the tw[o] types of lighting do not conflict. However, light as a rule [is] somewhat more expensive, because the installation is n[ot] cheap. You should gather information on this point fr[om] various manufacturers or importers. It is essential that t[he] cables are permanently installed; the switch is usua[lly] indoors. Choose the lamps with care and be sure to avo[id] artificial effects and ugly colours. A good garden lamp [is] unobtrusive.

Illumination in the garden need not cost so much. As [a] general rule pressed glass bulbs are used for this purpose, [as] these do not crack when rain hits a hot bulb. These bulbs a[re] available in 100 watt and 150 watt, both as spot-ligh[t] (9° cluster), floodlights (19° cluster) and wide-flood (2[?]° cluster). The cabling is fairly inexpensive. A convenie[nt] rubber extension system is available, which can be mov[ed] round the garden, so that you need only install a socket (w[ith] switch). The lamp fittings may be placed on pegs in t[he] garden or attached to wall-brackets.

Although in brochures individual lights are usually show[n] placed on pegs in the lawn, from where they illuminate t[he] borders, I do not advocate this system. The pegs get in t[he] way when you are maintaining the garden, and in the da[y]time they intrude. It is therefore much more sensible to pla[ce] the spotlights out of sight wherever possible, and to inst[all] them at a higher level, for instance on a fence. Try to crea[te]

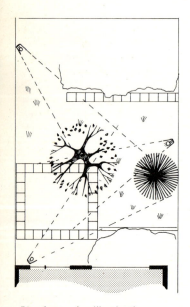

Plan for garden illumination

some counter-lighting; this gives better results. The sketch gives an example. A wide-beam floodlight on the house wall provides general foreground lighting. On the right a second floodlamp has been hidden behind a conifer, so that from the house you can see the light without having to look into the beam. The third light (a strong spotlight) is placed right at the bottom of the garden and skims the trees in a counter-direction. The cables should be placed out of sight as much as possible.

House and terrace in harmony

Our new housing estates often contain examples whe[re] house and garden do not harmonise. Why is this?

Everyone knows that there are good and bad architect[s] but most of them have had a thorough training and keep up to-date through their professional literature. The result [is] usually an up-to-date design. A garden designer could ha[ve] been employed as well, but unfortunately this is rarely th[e] case. In the majority of cases a garden is designed by [a] garden maintenance firm or a jobbing gardener, whos[e] experience is mainly confined to looking after the garden. [It] is not surprising that in such a case harmony between hous[e] and garden is frequently lacking, which seems rather a was[te] of money.

In the photograph on the facing page you can see how th[e] sober lines of a bungalow are reflected in the garden. Th[e] wooden terrace forms an attractive whole with the wa[ll] since the same material has been used for both, namely de[al] impregnated with a wood preserver stain. The constructi[on] of such a terrace is a fairly simple matter, not beyond th[e] capacity of a 'do-it-yourself' handyman. The sketch show[s] that the terrace is raised by means of concrete posts, whic[h] can be obtained anywhere; these are placed on bricks. [In] this way you can prevent the wood from rotting. The gard[en] itself, as far as it can be seen in the photograph, has bee[n] lowered about 25 cm (10 in.), which makes it look a[s] though the terrace floats above the stones. The soil remove[d] from here can be used to create a raised area beyond th[e] patio or elsewhere in the garden, possibly in the shape of [a] bank (see also page 105). These measures lower the gard[en] vis-à-vis the house and this always improves the perspectiv[e] in other words: the garden appears larger.

Whereas the terrace matches the material used round th[e] windows, the garden itself incorporates a greatly contrasti[ng] element, namely coarse pebbles. The tree in the foregroun[d] (a larch, to be exact) is, in fact, surrounded by a number [of] large stones. If you agree with me that this rough, age-o[ld] material looks well next to the clear lines of modern housin[g] there are ideas in plenty. Gravel in a more groomed form [is] found in the washed concrete slabs on which two orang[e] chairs have been placed. It is a good idea to lay these sla[bs] in strips; this also can to some extent create a spatial effe[ct].

The plants used should match the sober character of th[e] stones. The garden designer Plomin, from West German[y] used azaleas, rock plants and a larch. The plants in th[e] photograph are still very immature; at a later stage there w[ill]

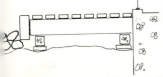

floating wooden terrace

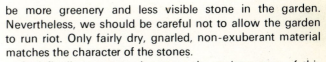

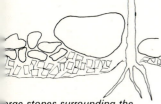

large stones surrounding the tree

be more greenery and less visible stone in the garden. Nevertheless, we should be careful not to allow the garden to run riot. Only fairly dry, gnarled, non-exuberant material matches the character of the stones.

And finally, a great advantage: the maintenance of this garden, which might justifiably be called a modern form of a rock garden, is restricted to the occasional removal of a few weeds.

The bottom of the garden

Somewhere the garden, or the lawn, comes to an end. This sounds obvious, but the solution is often less so. As a rule it goes something like this: oh, this is where we have to stop . . . or shall we go on a bit; or no, we can't . . . oh well let's leave it like this. It is true, isn't it, that the boundary posts are often visible through the vegetation? The grass grows in the border and the border in the lawn; there is no clear shape and after a time nothing remains of the design.

Have a look at the photograph. Here it is obvious where the lawn ends since it is edged on all sides by a narrow, but clearly defined border of washed tiles. This certainly facilitates lawn mowing, for in this case it is practically unnecessary to cut the edges. It also makes it easier to walk in the garden in wet weather or in winter. And finally such an edge clearly indicates where the grass ends, and if the design is well thought-out, the lawn thus shows to best advantage.

Next, the border beyond the lawn. The one illustrated has simply been raised 45 cm (18 in.), which not only greatly benefits the perennials, but which is also one of the best optical methods for finishing a garden. The edge is contained by a row of concrete sections (see pages 44, 65) with the open side in front. It can be used as a seat, rock plants spread over it cheerfully; it is an ideal solution. The soil which was dug out to lower the lawn is used behind the sections.

The border itself consists of red rose bushes, pink climbing roses and delphiniums in two shades of blue. Yellow and other colours are practically absent, which results in a peaceful and balanced combination. Immediately behind the border the garden is enclosed by tall shrubs.

Washed concrete steps and U-shaped elements are available from various firms. The flower pot is made of asbestos cement.

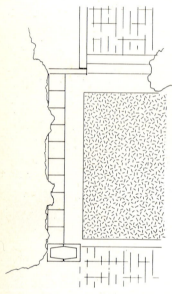

Plan of path, lawn edge and seating

A sandpit need not be ugly

You know how it usually goes: one Saturday Daddy says he will make a nice sandpit for the toddler. He does this by pushing a few posts into the ground, nailing four green painted planks to these, ordering some white sand – and there you have another of those monstrosities in the garden until after a year or two it happily collapses.

Perhaps, being a garden designer, I am particularly sensitive on this point, but surely with a little bit of goodwill it can be done properly! I wrote this book particularly to prove my point.

The photograph illustrates a perfectly simple example of logical design. The sandpit is situated fairly close to the terrace where father and mother are sunning themselves, so the toddler does not feel lonely. The sandpit can also be watched from the house beyond the lawn. The situation is a sunny one, and surely the plants growing round the pit can be nothing but an improvement. Perhaps it strikes you that the sandpit has been constructed in, and not on, the ground. On page 25 you will find another example of a sunken sand pit. There is a good reason for this. To begin with, a sunken pit is architectonically more attractive. Equally important is the fact that a child feels safer in a hollow than above ground level. Another advantage is that any spilled sand can simply be brushed back into the pit.

The method for constructing such a sandpit with the aid of railway sleepers is sketched on the left. A sleeper is usually 260 cm (8 ft 6 in.) in length; if you use the entire length, you will need eight (two layers), which make the interior of the sandpit approximately 200 × 200 cm (80 × 80 in.). If you want a smaller pit you will have to cut the sleepers. Place the ends of the sleepers on top of each other, as shown in the sketch, and use long nails to join them firmly. It is advisable to drill the wood first, otherwise you will never be able to get in the 17.5-cm (7-in.) nails required. It is a simple matter to make the junction with the tiles: put some sand underneath and use a spirit level.

Making a sandpit in a fibreglass pond is another good idea. Circular, square and oblong ponds are available, all with a 30-cm (12-in.) deeper area in the centre. A section may be seen on page 75 and elsewhere in this book. By filling only the deeper part with sand you provide a fine edge for the child's sandpies. As these ponds are waterproof, it is necessary to provide drainage to get rid of rainwater. If you select a situation which would be equally suitable for a

Construction of the pit

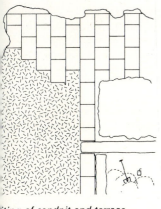

...ting of sandpit and terrace

pond, all you have to do when it is no longer wanted as a sandpit, is to remove the sand and fill the fibreglass mould with water.

The concrete sections shown on page 85 are also quite suitable for making a sandpit/pond. The possibilities are endless.

To keep cats out of the sandpit it is a good idea to make a lid for it. Do not make the planks too close fitting, for in that case the sand will dry out too much. A slatted lid, stained with a black wood preserver, is efficient and easy to lift when the sandpit is required.

And finally, while you are digging in any case, consider whether it would not be a good idea to have a tap near the sandpit; this might be useful for watering the garden as well. You can install this quite quickly yourself, using plastic tubing and union pieces.

Seating area below water level

A typical feature of the Dutch polders is that in som[e] places you can see shipping pass above eye-level. The pold[er] has been drained and the catch-water canals lie at a high[er] level.

In the patio garden illustrated on the facing page I hav[e] attempted to imitate this effect on a small scale. It is a matt[er] of a mere 10 cm (4 in.), but nevertheless it is pleasant to s[it] by a pool with a water level above the surrounding pave[ment]. In a large, landscaped garden it is a golden rule [to] have the pond — usually at groundwater level — in th[e] lowest place, but in small, artificially created gardens, suc[h] as this patio, there is no need to adhere to this rule.

When looking at the photograph you will be struck by th[e] use of red paving stones, unusual in a garden. These wer[e] used inside the bungalow and there were some left ove[r.] Although these paving stones cannot withstand frost an[d] will flake in the long run, we tried it all the same. For the sak[e] of economy they were laid loose on sand, which I would n[ot] really advise. They would look much better laid on a concre[te] foundation, and in that case, would probably withstan[d] frost better as well.

The pond is of the fibreglass type frequently used nowa[a]days, since concrete ponds have become too expensiv[e,] mainly because of labour costs. Fibreglass is moreover mor[e] waterproof. Sometimes these fibreglass pools have [a] beaded edge, which is not very attractive; as a rule they a[re] therefore surrounded by washed gravel tiles placed in such [a] way that they overhang the edge by about 7·5 cm (3 in.[)]

Since in this particular case we started with the pavin[g] stones (about 23 cm (9 in.) square), a different solution ha[d] to be found.

We began by constructing a 40-cm (16-in.) high wall [of] white limestone bricks, quite rough, but perfectly level at th[e] top; the beaded edge of the pond rests on this wall, whic[h] also ensure that it cannot subside. The paving stones cou[ld] then be set in mortar on the wall. Where the edge wa[s] visible, for instance opposite the seat, it was faced with th[e] paving stones as well. The seating area has been paved wi[th] 10 × 10 × 10 cm (4 × 4 × 4 in.) concrete bricks. Nowada[ys] these are available in a smaller size as well. Natural stor[e] would have been attractive, but these concrete cubes a[re] very much cheaper and their blue-black colour looks ver[y] well against the paving stones and the washed grave[l] slabs. The fine, smooth concrete seat is 170 × 44 cm (68 × 1[7] in.) and weighs 240 kg (528 lb).

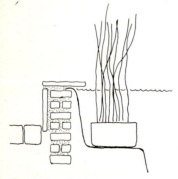

Pond edge finish

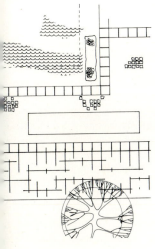

The water plants have been planted in fibreglass troughs, placed on the 30-cm (12-in.) wide and deep step of the pond, which gives them the correct 20-cm (8-in.) depth of water. Among the plants are irises and cat-tails. Pampas grass and spiderwort have been planted next to the pond. The small tree is an aralia and in the foreground you can see a young sumach or *Rhus typhina*.

A section of the lowered circular seating area is visible far right; this was constructed of the same bricks as the bungalow. Here, too, the paving consists of concrete cubes. In addition the garden contains a rock garden, a perennial border and a herb garden.

Pleasantly rough

The perfection and clean lines of modern architecture and interior design by contrast make many of us long for natural, wild, or at any rate rough garden. The photograph shows a section of such a garden. The house itself is of very advanced design (note the frame-less window and the roof construction), and the garden designer has consciously provided contrast, to my mind successfully.

Railway sleepers look very effective in the form of partition. Once the vine has spread, the wall will not require any maintenance.

The pavement of the terrace consists of granite stone arranged in a fairly irregular pattern. They are not exactly ideal for high heels, but their character suits the rough design. It does not matter if the grass grows among the stones; it need not be too tidy. The careless heap of pebbles on which a number of large stones have been placed, also goes well with the rest of the garden and enhances the contrast with the sober and tidy aspect of the house, which is clearly intended as a work of art. The fact that the vegetation, which consists of grasses such as *Festuca glauca* (low blue clumps) and a species of miscanthus (near the door), not very colourful is understandable. Violas or salvias would look quite wrong in this setting.

I do not know what the rest of the garden is like, but if I had any say in the matter, the terrace would be bordered by fairly rough lawn, full of daisies and speedwell, crossed by hardly visible path of granite stone leading to a lowered seating area at the bottom of the garden, constructed from horizontally placed and upright railway sleepers. A number of fruit trees would be planted in the grass, and near the seating area there would be a small pool, easily made by covering sheet of roofing felt or heavy plastic with a layer of pebbles. The hollow will hold water and there you have your pond, a drinking place for the birds.

There would be no bright colours anywhere, nor formal conifers; only mountain firs, larch and other rough trees. Such a garden would require very little maintenance and the pleasure it would give might be in reverse proportion!

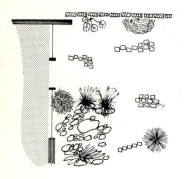

Plan of a rough terrace

Under a canopy

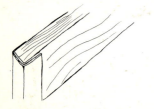

Junction of uprights and beams

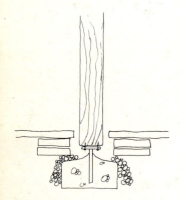

Rotproof installation of uprights

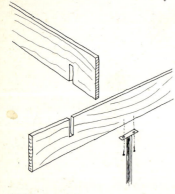

Linking sections

The pergola, or open corridor, has always played an important part in garden design. It feels pleasantly safe to walk underneath. Architectonically a pergola gives a garden more perspective and it is very suitable for optically linking two separate buildings (for instance house and garage). And finally, the pergola provides ideal growing conditions for the most beautiful climbers, such as vine, akebia, honeysuckle, roses, clematis, and many others.

Formerly pergolas were often made of painted wood, or even of concrete. Nowadays we look for long-lasting materials, requiring as little maintenance as possible. Impregnated poles are often used, but in my opinion such a rustic pergola is suitable only where the house is more or less in the same style. This is rarely the case in newly built structures and straightsided wood therefore looks better. Whether the pergola will be attractive or not will depend largely on the proportion between its length and width and the thickness of the wood, and on the proportions of the house.

In the photograph the measurements are in correct proportion. Steel profiles, anchored in concrete, have been used for the uprights (see sketch). They will have to be painted frequently. If you prefer wooden uprights, remember that they will start to rot at about 20 cm (8 in.) below ground. To prevent this happening I have worked out the construction shown in the second sketch. The wooden upright rests on a metal foot, anchored in concrete. The posts are surrounded by bricks, on which the terrace flags rest. To the eye it appears as if the posts continue straight into the ground; rainwater runs down into the holes and drains through the gravel. Even the metal remains relatively dry.

Where it is necessary to link sections of a pergola, it is advisable to do this by means of deep incisions in the wood. The junction can be reinforced with waterproof glue or a nail.

Ordinary deal may be used for pergolas, but this is less straight than the more expensive kinds of wood. In addition it has to be treated with a preservative at regular intervals, which is of course quite difficult when the pergola is densely overgrown. For this reason you should certainly consider constructing the pergola from a weatherproof wood, such as cedar, possibly a tropical hardwood, perhaps even oak. Weatherproof wood which has not been treated with a preservative will turn a beautiful grey in the course of time.

Vegetables and herbs on the balcony

Not only herbs, but vegetables as well, can easily be grow on a sheltered balcony — good news for people without garden. If you want to make it look attractive, the phot graph on the facing page may give you some ideas. T containers have been tested in a garden, but can of cour equally well be placed on a balcony. The attractive and us ful wooden sections (also ideal for making compost) c quickly be put together or taken down, and can be made high as you like. The way they are constructed is shown the sketch. It seems to me that any but the most clum persons would be able to saw a number of planks to t required depth, afterwards knocking out the small notch with a chisel. If you possess a circular saw, you simply ma two cuts. The wood can be ordered to size. Deal is perfec adequate, but of course a more lasting type of wood, such Western Red Cedar, would look more attractive.

These containers are filled with compost, which can bought ready mixed. In principle any desired vegetable c be grown. Sow some herbs in between, so that the space well filled. Smaller, plastic containers are also very suitab as can be seen in the photograph. A recently develope dwarf tomato 'Pixie' can be grown quite simply in bucke sized containers.

A good supply of water and nourishment is essential; t quicker a plant grows, the more nourishment it require Organic manure is best for growing food. A mixture dried blood, bone meal and wood ash makes a good a round fertiliser for this purpose.

Naturally other containers may be used as well. Halve beer barrels, wooden tubs, asbestos cement containers — these are useful for growing annual plants, which will n suffer from frost damage. For a choice of vegetables a herbs you should consult a good plant catalogue.

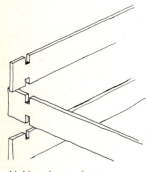

Linking the sections

Plants are personalities

If you look at plants carefully you will find that each has certain personality, a well-defined individual charact Their true nature is often partially lost after endless crossi and unusual treatments, such as atomic radiation – su nonsense! At times, however, crossing may strengthen plant's character; this is the case, for instance, with certa roses.

If the above strikes a chord, you will agree with me that v fail to respect the character of plants if we use them 'colour-areas' or 'garden-filling'. On the other hand we c show a plant respect by giving it a carefully selected situati in the garden. This is, of course, not an easy subject discuss, because everyone will see it differently. But there such an enormous choice of plants that it enables you to creative.

I believe that this has happened in the garden illustrat on the facing page. Just see how freely the blue delphiniu grows in the background. It is allowed to show itself fro top to toe, including its bare stems. And don't you think th the roses in the foreground have been combined in a beau fully light manner with catmint *(Nepeta)* and lavenc *(Lavandula)*? The border has not been crammed w plants; each one shows to full advantage and – mc important – they complement each other instead of clashin The latter is something that often strikes me, where plants totally different character have been placed next to ea other. They do not *like* each other and the quarrel betwe them fills the entire garden with discord. In the gard illustrated I do not get that feeling, but you may see differently.

The photograph and the text, therefore, are purely effort to make you think about the individuality of eve plant. I believe that everyone who has the slightest creati instinct will enjoy enormously playing with them. In th connection an inborn feeling for plants is more importa than acquired knowledge. But you should begin by sheddir false notions such as: 'it isn't done' or 'it's impossible'.

A suspended staircase and a pond

And all that in solid concrete, but . . . constructed entire of ready-made sections. As you see, a very great deal can l achieved with garden stone or U-shaped sections.

What these sections look like is clearly shown in the photographs on the facing page and elsewhere, as well as the sketches. In order to place them easily and perfect level, I would advise you to start by laying a simple concret foundation. The sketch shows how this can best be done.

With the aid of posts, two battens are placed horizontal on a firmly stamped soil base. The distance between the tw battens can be slightly smaller than the length of the concrete section. Mortar, which you can easily mix yourse is now poured between the planks. Reinforcement is usual unnecessary. The concrete layer is about 10 cm (4 in.) thic that is, the height of the battens. While still wet, the mortar levelled with a straight slat, so that the surface becomes nice and smooth. When all the foundations have been laid, the elements can be placed. This can be done by scattering very thin layer of white sand on the foundations, but ensure that the sections are firmly fixed, I would advise a 1– cm ($\frac{1}{2}$–$\frac{3}{4}$ in.) layer of mortar. Place the sections as accurate as possible, using a spirit level and a rubber hammer.

The sketch shows how the foundations underneath th sections have been placed in such a way that steps a formed. If the open sides are facing forward, it will look as the steps are floating on air. To make them easy to walk o you should employ the staircase formula, that is: tread 2 × height of rise = length of pace. The tread is the depth the steps, which in the case of these sections is 40 or 45 c (16 or 18 in.), depending on the make. The riser is the heigh of the step, and this you can determine yourself. Length o pace differs with individual people, but varies betwee 65 cm (26 in.) (small women) and 75 cm (30 in.) (men). you want to know the length of your own pace exactly, yo need only walk a few steps in recently raked sand. If th length of your pace is 70 cm (28 in.), then the riser for 40-c (16-in.) deep sections should be 15 cm (6 in.) (40 + (2 × 15 = 70), and for 45-cm (18-in.) sections 12$\frac{1}{2}$ cm (5 in.).

A word about the pool, which has been constructed of th same sections. I hope you will be able to see from the sketc how this is done. First a concrete lining was made, with deeper section in the centre (for water-lilies and for goldfis in winter). The sections were then erected in mortar on to of this layer. For the corners special sections have to be mad to order. To make everything watertight I used a quick

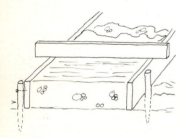

Levelling concrete foundations

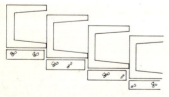

U-shaped elements forming steps

84

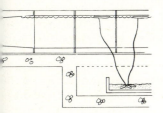

Section of pool construction

hardening seam filling compound which was squirted between the gaps at the time of erection. Provided you work accurately, the result will be watertight.

Of course it would be a pity if such a pool were to freeze in winter. For that reason a small electric underwater pump has been incorporated, which should be kept switched on at any rate during periods of frost. The photograph does not show very clearly that half the pool is sunk into the ground. This is not essential, but in this case it looked better, since the pool forms the centre of a large sunken seating area made of the same sections. A part of the seating is visible to right and left of the steps in the photograph.

A mobile garden

Example of a mobile garden

Why should a balcony garden always be confined to a trough-shaped box attached to the railing and containing the inevitable African marigolds? No, no, a thousand times no. You can do much more with flower boxes, especially if the balcony is of reasonable size. You should attempt, however, to make everything movable, so that you can take it with you if you have to move.

Large fibreglass or asbestos-cement boxes offer the widest possibilities. The photograph shows how they can be combined at different levels into a kind of miniature garden. Each box can be filled with the most suitable soil (acid soil for heathers, limey soil for rock plants such as sempervivums, etc.), which is a great advantage. Make sure that there are drainage holes in each box, and provide a good layer of drainage material. It is quite possible to grow trees in the larger boxes, and one or more boxes may be turned into small ponds. Wooden tubs and large Provençal terra cotta pots add variety to the work of your mobile garden.

rass green

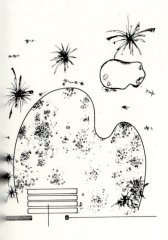

*rnamental grasses round a
ebble pond*

A garden full of grass — not a mown lawn, but a variety of grasses which have been allowed to grow freely. Large groups of low, creeping grasses, such as *Festuca*, with here and there a clump of tall, loose grasses, for instance ornamental oats *(Helictotrichon sempervirens)*, or the proud and loftily swaying pampas grass *(Cortaderia selloana)*. Grasses which are beautiful in spring, when they burst from the soil full of vigour, such as *Miscanthus sinensis*, or clumps which turn a magnificent red-brown towards winter, for instance molinia (left in the photograph).

There is a tremendous choice in grasses, and in a garden which contains nothing else flowers are hardly missed. Many grasses are perennials and they vary in height between 10 cm (4 in.) and 3 m (10 ft) *(Miscanthus sacchariflorus* or *Arundo donax)*. They look best combined with natural stone, scattered rocks, or possibly railway sleepers. If you do not know anything about grasses, why not order the entire assortment and experiment? It will not cost you more than about £15 and a year of your garden's time.

Create space in your garden

Nowadays, unfortunately, gardens can rarely be larg[e] since in most areas land has become too expensive. For th[is] reason we should, in designing and planting our garden[s] try to make them look larger by means of optical illusion. T[o] my mind this is no less justifiable than carefully choosing [a] dress or suit which will make you look younger.

Every good garden designer has a few tricks up his sleev[e] which he guards as if they were industrial secrets. A few [of] these are disclosed in this book; one of them is the knowledg[e] that partitioning creates space. A garden appears larger if [it] is divided into different sections or spaces, leading into eac[h] other, but not all visible from one angle. This principle [is] clearly demonstrated in the design by C. Wegener illustrate[d] here. It is quite an old-fashioned concept, for designers [of] previous eras used the same method to make the parks [of] their day appear even larger. Your glance follows the curve[d] line up to the point where it turns away. The next fixed poir[t] lies beyond the green carpet of the lawn, a distance difficu[lt] to estimate (see the dotted lines). At that moment yo[u] experience a sensation of space which is partly a visu[al] trick.

These curved lines are often seen nowadays in the artles[s] gardens laid out by many a jobbing gardener. You kno[w] them: a tiny, shapeless lawn in the centre, edged by a care[-] fully raked border, in which the season starts with bulbou[s] plants, to be followed by African marigolds and salvias. T[o] my mind this is the lowest form of garden. In these cases th[e] curved lines have no function, since the curves are not dee[p] enough to create the optical illusion described above.

In the garden illustrated, which is not exactly small, b[ut] not enormous either, the ancient principle was once mor[e] used to good effect. From no single point can the entir[e] garden be seen at a glance: one has the feeling that there [is] much more to it than meets the eye. And this is indeed th[e] case. To achieve this effect you should make sure that th[e] lawn is *narrow in the centre*. The borders should jut out we[ll] into the grass. If you understand this trick, the rest wi[ll] follow, especially if you lower the lawn by 10—20 cm (4— [8] in.) and use the soil dug out in the borders, as was don[e] here.

The shape of the lawn can be attractively and cleverl[y] accentuated by the use of natural stone. This is useful als[o] for lawn mowing. The stone edge could easily be mad[e] wider. By mowing in a certain way, using a machine with [a] roller, you can create lines in the grass which heighten th[e]

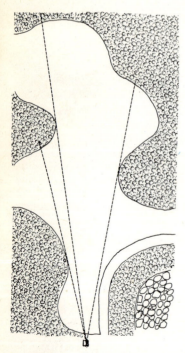

Sightlines in the garden illustrated

design. Another good idea is the curved path leading out of the picture on the right.

If you do not like this kind of garden you should remember that the same effect may be achieved with straighter lines. The main thing is the creation of wings out of sight, giving an illusion of depth. At the same time you should consider the use of slender plants, such as grasses, in the foreground. This is another trick for creating the appearance of space — very important in modern gardens.

A border from a seed packet

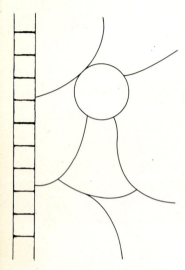

Plan for a border grown from seed

Sowing in rows

As a rule, borders are built up with the aid of perennials often in combination with shrubs. It is, however, quite possible to make a border consisting entirely of annuals. As the word implies, such a border will give pleasure for one season only, but it is inexpensive, growth will be exuberant and the layout will not involve as much work as you might think. The result, about three months after sowing, is illustrated on the facing page. This photograph was taken in the garden of the Royal Horticultural Society, Wisley.

In annual borders the seed is usually sown *in situ*. You start by making a plan, which might look like the sketch on the left. Be careful not to make the sections too small. Choose strong, abundantly- and long-flowering species which do not require staking, for example eschscholzia love-in-a-mist *(Nigella)*, coreopsis sweet alyssum *(Lobularia)*, snapdragons *(Antirrhinum)*, cornflowers *(Centaurea)*, annual delphinium, tobacco plants *(Nicotiana)*, toadflax *(Linaria)*, marigolds *(Calendula)*, gypsophila, asters *(Callistephus)*, African Marigolds *(Tagetes)* and many others.

When consulting a book on the subject of flowers grown from seed, or – better still – a detailed catalogue, you should look under the heading for annual plants which can be grown *in situ*. Try to combine the colours in an attractive way and make sure that the lowest plants are sown in front. Ornamental grasses can also be used effectively. The only thing which might spoil your success is a superfluity of weeds. It is therefore necessary to prepare the seedbed well in advance (rake to a very fine tilth) and to remove the weeds which come up by means of hoeing, or better still, by burning them off. Manuring is not advisable, since this would make the plants grow too fast and liable to collapse.

Just before sowing, towards the end of April, you copy the lines of the sketch in the border with the upper end of your rake. You then draw furrows to a depth of 2 cm ($\frac{3}{4}$ in.) in each section and tip in the seeds straight from the packet. *Be sure to sow plentifully*, otherwise the whole thing will be a failure. As the seed will come up in rows, it will be easy to distinguish the weeds, so that you will be able to do some weeding in June, at the same time thinning where necessary. Once the border is covered in growth, the rows will be invisible and you will have a sea of flowers.

The dominating verbascum

On page 82 I philosophised a little about the character c plants. The accompanying photograph shows that a few we chosen plants need not sacrifice their natures, but can remai themselves while complementing each other.

In the photograph on the facing page you can see how single plant can dominate an entire garden at a certain tim of the year. Just try to imagine this garden without the ta yellow Mullein *(Verbascum olympicum)*. All that remain is pebbles and a few plants which at this particular momer are hardly exuberant.

This verbascum is a self-seeding biennial. Most of th young plants should be removed (otherwise they would fi the entire garden), but some of them should be planted in carefully selected spot — a different one each year.

There are several other biennials of this kind, the bes known being the foxglove *(Digitalis)*. Honesty *(Lunaria* can also be very beautiful (try it in front of a scarlet flowerin currant), while no real garden lover should do withou hollyhocks *(Althaea)*, although these are less easy to grow

If we look for perennials with character and style, th first plant to come to mind would be the giant hogwee *(Heracleum mantegazzianum)*. This plant requires damp fertile soil and some shade. The equally large *Gunner manicata* or giant rhubarb could spread over an entire sma garden, provided it has a damp situation. Much bette known are the ornamental grasses such as the frequentl used pampas grass *(Cortaderia)*. Among the extremel attractive specimen trees I would mention birches (especi ally species with beautiful bark), maples such as *Ace griseum, A. capillipes*, etc., which also have fine bark; th relatively rare southern beech *(Nothofagus)* with its typica fernlike branching; the frequently used sumach *(Rhus,* which can grow very rapidly; the sweet gum *(Liquidambar,* particularly conspicuous in winter; possibly a weepin wych elm *(Ulmus glabra* 'Pendula'*)*.

I have seen gardens which contained nothing but bam boos *(Arundinaria japonica; A. murieliae)*, and gravel. It atmosphere was very pleasant and maintenance, of course was minimal.

Experiment with something different; try to make particu lar plants dominate and you will achieve a garden which i distinctive and not commonplace.

Terrace enclosed by pond

A lot can be done with water in the garden — more than generally thought. Page 41 shows how an entire house can be surrounded by a kind of moat. In the case illustrated here the designer has not gone quite so far: the pool marks the end of part of the garden, namely the terrace, and via two stepping stones gives access to another part: the lawn.

Used in this manner, as a boundary, water has an obvious function and this is how I like it being used. Other places where water might be used as a boundary are: between lowered seating area and a terrace; between garden and road (in that case it would really be a sort of ditch); between house and garden. The most sensible place for a pond is next to a seating area, because the fascinating pond-life can be observed only from nearby.

If you look at the photograph again you will notice that as is the case with other pools described in this book, the partition between lawn and water is constructed of a hard material, in this case a washed concrete edge or step. Not only does this look better, but it is also more practical than having grass growing up to the edge of the pool, for in that case a great deal of grass would fall into the water during mowing, and the edge would have to be trimmed by hand.

Only in the case of large, natural ponds does a lawn continuing to the edge of the water look well. In such a case the partition usually consists of a brick lining. Pools such as the one illustrated are as a rule still made of concrete, since fibreglass pools are available in certain sizes only. However modular pools are now available, measuring 360 × 155 cm (144 × 62 in.), with a maximum depth of 60 cm (24 in.). Several of these may be linked, though a narrow edge will remain visible. These ponds are not cheap, but nevertheless compare favourably with concrete constructions. Do-it-yourself experts can make a fibreglass pond themselves. A rough shape is made in concrete, smoothed with plaster. One might even use chipboard, shaping the rounded corner with plaster. Another method is to make a basic shape of hessian soaked in plaster. The actual pond is then constructed by adding several layers of polyester and fibreglass. Such a construction is so strong that it will not matter if the basic shape rots. Fibreglass pools cannot break as a result of freezing. Concrete pools have to be kept frost-free during winter, for instance by operating a small pump in frosty weather.

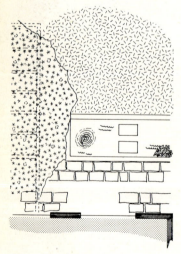

Plan of terrace, pool and lawn

Wall climbers

A house as a rule looks much more inviting if part of it
covered with climbers. On new estates, especially, climbe
can give a house a great deal more atmosphere.

It is often feared that a climber will damage the structur
Ivy *(Hedera)* has a particularly bad reputation in this respe
It is true that aerial roots will penetrate poor mortar, but o
the other hand a covered wall remains dry, which in its tu
lengthens the life-span. It really is not true that ruins ha
fallen into decay because they were covered in ivy. Ten
one there would be no ruins left at all if it were not for the iv
Hedera colchica 'Paddy's Pride', illustrated opposite, is a
ivy which will certainly not run riot over your house. Th
variegated white form is called 'Dentata Variegata'.

The Virginia creeper, *Parthenocissus quinquefolia*,
deciduous shrub, is self-clinging like the ivy, with which it
often confused. In the autumn its foliage colour changes
magnificent shades of red. The common species, the Bosto
ivy, is called *P. tricuspidata* and has three-lobed leave
whereas *P. quinquefolia* is five-lobed.

The Dutchman's pipe, *Aristolochia macrophylla* has ve
decorative heart-shaped foliage and will thrive in shade. Th
less well-known five-lobed *Akebia quinata* has a gracef
growth habit and can easily reach a height of 10 m (33 f
Both these plants require support.

A fine wall covering is provided by *Hydrangea petiolar*
which not only has beautiful foliage, but flowers as we
Grow this against a north wall and provide support.

Among the best known wall climbers are climbing rose
clematis and honeysuckle *(Lonicera)*. The first two requi
sun, but honeysuckle tolerates a great deal of shade. Suppo
is essential. Finally I should mention the beautiful wistar
which is, however, slightly less easy to grow.

When planting wall climbers it is of the greatest importan
that you dig a very large hole, to the depth of the hou
foundations. Clematis in particular benefits from th
treatment, but so, undoubtedly, do the others. Close to t
wall the soil usually consists of rubble and sand, a mixtu
which is not very attractive to hungry roots.

The planting hole — the larger the better — is filled with
mixture of garden peat or peat fibre, rough stable manu
compost and some good garden soil. When this mixture h
settled, the climber can be planted and trained along hoo
or wires attached to the wall. I prefer plastic wall-plugs, in
which I screw brass eyelet-screws, to which plastic wire ca
be attached.

Improving the soil for a climber

A modern terrace

This terrace could well serve as a text book example of
modern seating area, full of atmosphere. Its lay-out, use c
materials and furnishings create a tranquil effect, while at th
same time it contrasts well with the fairly wild garden beyonc
Let us see how this construction was achieved.

The photographer had his back to the house. Beyond th
small pool you can just see a post of the pergola, the othe
side of which is attached to the wall of the house. Across th
terrace we look out into the garden, where an amusin
spherical garden lamp is visible among the numerous plants
The terrace has been constructed of natural flagstone
which have probably been used in the house as well. Thi
fact, combined with the sheltering pergola, strengthens th
impression of a 'garden room'. The transition from house t
garden is gradual, not abrupt.

As it would be a pity to lay expensive natural stone slab
straight on to sand (they are very thin and would thus brea
easily), a concrete foundation has been laid, leaving
square space free for the pool. The concrete has bee
reinforced with wire mesh. The hole for the pond need not b
watertight (this would require a very thick and properl
made concrete floor), for at a later stage it can be covered i
polyester/fibreglass.

The concrete floor has a gradient of approximately 2 cr
($\frac{3}{4}$ in. per yd) per m, so that all the rainwater runs away fror
the house. The natural stone slabs are firmly fixed in a 2-cr
($\frac{3}{4}$-in.) layer of cement mortar. The simple low woode
fence at the edge of the terrace is an attractive idea; it seem
as if the designer wanted to indicate: this is where the garde
begins.

Why, you may ask, was it thought necessary to place
basin *on top* of the pool? Probably the designer felt that th
design lacked contrast in levels; he wanted to make the wat
more prominent and therefore raised it a little. At the sam
time this created an opportunity for introducing an interest
ing sound of splashing water, since the water now fal
twice: first from the sprinkler and then over the edge
the basin.

Of course the modern furniture contributes greatly to th
up-to-date effect of the terrace. We all know that plasti
chairs are not as comfortable as all that, because they do n
'give'. But they are perfectly adequate for breakfast and tha
is exactly what I should like to suggest: have breakfast o
this pleasant terrace, with the birds actively occupied in th
garden and the sun just peeping in under the pergola. Th

an of terrace

ection of the pond

chairs and the table can be left outside all the year round, which is a great advantage. A wipe with a damp cloth and they will be as good as new.

Here are a few tips if you want to build such a terrace yourself. Begin by buying the washed concrete basin and adapt the dimensions of the pond to this. The section sketch shows that the basin has been raised on stones in the pond. A hole will have to be made in the base to accommodate the pipe of the fountain, and this should be sealed with an adhesive filler. The small pump can be bought from any good garden centre. Away from the pool the cable can be hidden by some large stones. To avoid damage in winter, the pump should be switched on in cold weather. This kind of pond is not suitable for goldfish or plants.

Vigour from the compost heap

I am not exaggerating when I tell you that you can gi[ve] your plants vitality by turning house- and garden-refuse in[to] compost. You need not confine yourself to weeds from t[he] garden, dead twigs, organic kitchen garbage and dustba[in] from the vacuum cleaner: even things such as cardboa[rd] boxes (preferably unprinted) can be used in the mixture a[nd] will be turned into useful compost within a short space [of] time. It's not true that it will smell; in fact, properly process[ed] refuse will have a pleasant leafmould smell. The process tak[es] six to twelve months. Come and have a look at my garden [if] you don't believe me! Since an unfenced heap looks unti[dy] and takes up too much room in a small garden, I wou[ld] advise you to buy a container, or to build one as shown in t[he] photograph. Better to build a double one, while you're at [it,] to create a constant process. Each container should [be] 80 × 80 × 80 or 100 × 100 × 100 cm (32 × 32 × 32 or 40 [×] 40 × 40 in.). They are available in galvanised iron, concrete [or] plastic; you can build them yourself of bricks or of concre[te] blocks. The containers illustrated have been constructed [of] precast blocks glued together – ideal for people who la[ck] expertise in working with mortar. Openings have been le[ft] between the bricks, to admit air. The front has been finish[ed] with loose boards, dropped into grooves. The boards are ke[pt] apart by partly inserted screws.

Composting starts by dumping a 15–20 cm (6–8 in) layer of well mixed refuse in the container, sprinkled wi[th] about 57 g (2 oz) of dried blood. This material is forked in[to] the refuse. You then cover the mixture with some garde[n] soil, preferably loam, but ordinary soil will do, and put [on] another layer of refuse, which is in turn sprinkled wi[th] hydrated lime, and soil added as before. Subsequent laye[rs] are treated in exactly the same manner. When the contain[er] is full, you leave it for a further couple of months, befo[re] transferring the semi-composted material to the secon[d] container, again mixing it with dried blood and lime, but th[is] time using only half the quantities mentioned above. T[he] first container is now ready to receive fresh refuse. After [a] few months, six at most, you can sieve the contents of t[he] second container and use them. Compost may be used [all] through the late spring and summer, but the best time [to] apply it is in October. Just scatter it over the soil and repe[at] every year, especially under trees, shrubs, etc. You w[ill] never have to use artificial fertilisers or stable manure aga[in.]

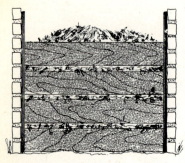

Compost container, front view

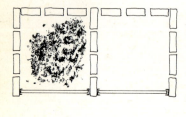

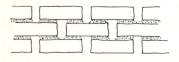

Detail of construction and containers seen from above

Keeping out the dogs

A house with a front garden nearly always has a low fenc[e], little more than an indication of the boundary and a barri[er] to the eye, but it also keeps passing dogs from spending [a] penny on your crocuses. A close fence, on the other han[d], would serve better to keep bits of paper from blowing int[o] your garden.

We can therefore agree about the usefulness of such a lo[w] boundary fence, but possibly you would like to improve i[ts] appearance. In my opinion very low fences often do n[o]t suit the style of the house.

For instance, those senselessly curved pine wood plank[s], often varnished into the bargain, look extremely ugly i[n] front of a severely modern bungalow. Why not use a slende[r] flat strip of wood, fixed to flat hardboard posts? See th[e] sketch. Stain the wood very dark brown and attach a glas[s] brick with your house number to it. If you find that you a[re] troubled by paper blowing in from the street, fix som[e] blackened wire netting to the inside.

If you are prepared to spend a little more money, a bric[k] wall is practical and lasting. The sketch gives an impressio[n] of a wall made of three layers of square black concret[e] blocks, $15 \times 15 \times 15$ cm ($6 \times 6 \times 6$ in.). They should b[e] cemented with black mortar. Remember that the foundatio[n] should be at frost-free level, that is, at least 60 cm (24 in.[)].

Somewhat higher fencing can be bought ready-made i[n] various forms. They usually consist of metal posts an[d] bearers, to which boards are attached. The metal has bee[n] give a plastic coating, so that it is reasonably rust-proo[f]. These fences are supplied in kits and can be erected by an[y] do-it-yourself handyman. As the posts are not very tall, it [is] advisable to mount them in concrete, or at least to fill th[e] holes with rubble, otherwise your nice fence will soon b[e] wrecked by carelessly playing children, and that would b[e] bad for your blood pressure.

If you have experience in welding, you might make [a] fence to your own design; an example is shown in th[e] photograph. You can give free rein to your fantasy.

The photograph on page 99 shows that a fence may als[o] have its uses in the middle of the garden, for instance as a[n] optical as well as factual partition between flower garden an[d] vegetable garden. However, we should aim at a partitio[n] which suits the garden and does not look out of place o[r] pointless.

If you want to cover a low fence, there are various plant[s] suitable for the purpose. In the thirties climbing roses wer[e]

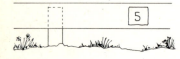

Straight board partition

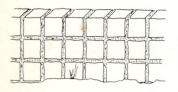

Low wall of square bricks

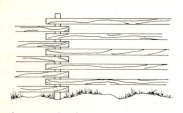

Low wooden fence

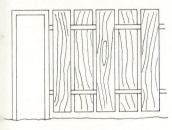

Horizontal fencing kit

Vertical fencing kit

generally used. The common ivy *(Hedera)* also looks well. A climbing hydrangea *(Hydrangea petiolaris)* can be kept pruned and will look charming. *Vitis coignetiae*, a large-leaved ornamental vine, and the early-flowering *Clematis montana rubens* which has small rose-pink flowers, are two further unusual possibilities.

Create an illusion of size

In the course of time garden designers have developed number of tricks to make gardens appear larger than the really are. They are all based on optical illusion and I believ this is fully justified. We do exactly the same in our homes On page 88 I have discussed the creation of space by mean of division. In this chapter you will find some tips for en larging your garden by differences in level.

You may have noticed abroad, or in hilly parts of this country, that sloping gardens appear much larger than leve ones. Of course if measured on the level, a 100 sq m (100 sc yd) slope is larger than a 100 sq m (100 sq yd) area of leve ground, but in addition a slope creates space by being terraced. Level sections interspersed with banks togethe appear larger than a gradual, unbroken slope. Well-knowr photographs of rice fields in Bali provide a good example Exactly the same effect may be achieved in an originally leve garden. A lowered seating area need only be 20–40 cm (8–16 in.) deep to create considerable effect. Anothe method is to lay the lawn on a slightly lower level than the surrounding flowerbeds. This may be done by making the borders slope gently upwards, but another effective methoc is the construction, around the lawn, of a 30–50 cm (12–2C in.) high bank, which may consist of concrete elements. Several examples are illustrated in this book.

In the garden shown in the photograph on the facing page the lawn rises slightly at the farther end. I am not sure who discovered this trick, but it is certainly frequently and successfully used in Germany to create an illusion of size. The effect is due to the fact that the boundary of the garden is hidden. It looks as though the garden continues for a considerable distance behind the bank, but in actual fact there is at most 2 m (2 yd) of vegetation behind the highest point of the slope, followed by a steep drop to the boundary (see sketch). The soil needed for the creation of the bank can be taken from the lawn area. A mechanical shovel can do this in a few hours, but choose very dry weather for the job and be careful that the soil does not become too hard.

When making banks in a lawn you should take into consideration that they must be easy to mow. If the junction between the level area and the gradient is made too abrupt, the mower will 'bite', or cut too high. Since these things depend on the type of lawn-mower used, it is advisable to experiment with the machine before you start sowing, to see how the bank should slope. Rather higher banks are nowadays often used in gardens on roads with busy traffic, for

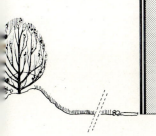

ction of the garden illustrated

nothing keeps out noise better than a solid earth wall. If you construct a lowered seating area just below, you will keep out a considerable amount of noise.

When planting banks it should be remembered that the soil will be much drier there. We should select trees which are proof against such conditions, for example birches, rowan trees, hawthorns, possibly maples, flowering currants, etc.

A distinguished drive

The way a garden or a patio is paved can be of immens importance in creating an impression. You may have see examples in Italy or Spain of the effect that may be achieve by means of natural stone laid in a mosaic pattern. Th attractive interplay of lines creates an intimate impression.

I have selected the photograph on the opposite page prove the effect that may be achieved with stone mosaic in private garden. The photograph shows the junction betwee the garage and the road, an area of about 6×7 m (7×8 yd In other words: a drive, which has to satisfy certain require ments. It should be comfortable to walk and drive on, lo attractive and possibly create a dignified impression, for it visible from the road and is in constant use, both by yourse and by others.

The drive illustrated meets all these requirements and it moreover, original and fascinating in design.

The only disadvantage of such a drive is that it is n cheap. Natural stone is expensive, since it has to be individ ally cut by hand, and imported from a distance. On the oth hand, it will not wear out and will look equally attractive two hundred years' time, something that can hardly be sa of concrete. The drive will therefore increase the value of t house and consequently should be regarded as an inves ment rather than as an expense.

The following are some of the materials suitable for th purpose:
yellow limestone
green porphyry
pink-grey porphyry
black diabase
red granite
medium grey granite
white granite
ochre granite
white dolomite

All these materials are available from specialist firms, b some are quite rare. Occasionally one might be able to buy secondhand lot of stones from roads that are being renewe but as a rule these are too large.

To have the stones laid you would do best to approach old road-maker, a man who loves his job and might willing to help you in his spare time. Perhaps you would able to prepare the base yourself. This consists of a 15 c (6 in.) layer of coarse rubble, a 5–10 cm (2–4 in.) layer

fine rubble and finally a 5 cm (2 in.) layer of fine sand. The rubble must be thoroughly rammed down, which can be done with a hand-stamper or with a mechanical rammer. Do not allow yourself to be tempted to lay such expensive material on an insufficiently prepared base; this will only result in subsidence. A good result can only be achieved on a perfectly drained base, which is created by rubble.

To ensure that no puddles can remain on the pavement, even when, after a few years' time, the seams have filled in, it is advisable to make a gradient of 3–4 cm ($1\frac{1}{4}$–$1\frac{3}{4}$ in.) per metre. A drive usually slopes towards the road, so in this case there is no problem.

A pleasant terrace

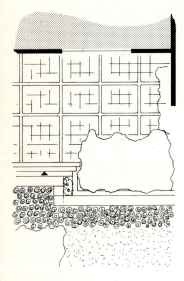

Plan of the terrace

The garden designer Christian Wegener achieved an attractive connection between terrace and garden for a house-in-a-row. The garden was lowered approximately 30–40 cm (12–16 in.), which created pleasantly contrasting levels. The junction between the levels is formed by a cheerfully planted bank and washed concrete steps, which can be bought ready-made.

The terrace itself has also been constructed from washed concrete slabs, joined by bricks (see sketch). The photograph shows how the concrete slabs merge into a pavement of wooden discs. This, in turn, could border the lawn.

I should just like to comment on the sunshade, which in this case clashes with the garden. This is a point which is often overlooked, as is the colour of garden chairs, etc. In many cases, although by no means always, bright blue is the best colour.

INDEX